Aristotle's Metaphysical and Scientific Masterpieces

A Exploration of Reality, Perception, and the Forces That Shape Our World

A Modern Translation

Adapted for the Contemporary Reader

Translated by Tim Zengerink

Table of Contents

PREFACE

MESSAGE TO THE READER

Dear Reader,

Thank you for choosing this edition; it is more than just a book—you are reading a living thread of humanity's literary heritage.

We'd like to invite you to **gain immediate, unlimited digital & audiobook access** to hundreds of the most treasured literary classics ever written—along with the option to **secure deluxe paperback, hardcover & box set editions at printing cost**. Together, we can **spark a new global literary renaissance** alongside our small, independent publishing house called "The Library of Alexandria."

Thousands of years ago, the Library of Alexandria stood as a beacon of knowledge—until it was lost to history. We aim to reignite that spirit of preservation and discovery right now, in the modern age—only this time, it's accessible to all, in every language and every format.

Picture a world where every timeless classic, novel, poem, or philosophical treatise is not only available to read but also updated for today's readers—modernized, translated into any language or dialect, and ready to enjoy in any format you choose, whether that is in an eBook, audiobook, paperback, or deluxe hardcover & box set version a printing cost.

By joining our movement to **rebuild the modern Library of Alexandria**, you become part of an unprecedented mission to offer:

- **Unlimited Audiobook & eBook Access to the Greatest Classics of All Time**

  Instantly explore thousands of legendary works, from Plato and Shakespeare to Jane Austen and Leo Tolstoy. All are instantly ready to read or listen to, giving you a complete literary universe at your fingertips.

- **Paperback & Deluxe Editions at Printing Costs:**

  Purchase any title in a paperback, deluxe hardbound, or deluxe boxset edition at printing costs, shipped right to your doorstep. Curate your personal library of Alexandria with editions worthy of display—crafted to last, designed to captivate, and delivered straight to your door.

- **Modern translations for Contemporary Readers in all languages and dialects**

  Discover a vast selection of classics reimagined in clear, current language—no more struggling with outdated phrases or obscure references. Next to the original versions, we aim to offer translations in as many languages and dialects as possible.

As we continue our translation efforts and add new languages, readers everywhere can connect with these works as if they were written today. ***By bridging linguistic divides, you're contributing to ensuring that these timeless stories become more meaningful, accessible, and inspiring for people across the globe.***

- **Your Personal Library of Alexandria:**

  Over the months and years, you'll curate a unique physical archive of classics—each volume a testament to your taste, curiosity, and love of knowledge. It's not just about owning books—it's about curating a cultural legacy you'll cherish and pass down for generations to come.

- **Join a Global Literary Renaissance:**

  Your support fuels an ongoing mission: allowing us to reinvest in offering deluxe print editions (including special boxsets) at their true cost, broaden the range of available formats and translations, and extend the reach of these works to new audiences worldwide. By joining today, you're not just preserving a legacy of masterpieces; ***you set in motion a powerful wave of literary accessibility.***

We are more than a publisher—we're a movement, and we can't do it alone. Your support lets us scale our mission, preserving and reimagining history's greatest works for tomorrow's readers.

Become a Torchbearer of knowledge.

Thank you for picking up this book and allowing us into your literary journey. As you turn the pages, know that you're part of something larger: a global effort to keep these stories alive, share their wisdom across borders and generations, and spark a true cultural revival for the modern era.

If this resonates with you—please consider taking the next step. By visiting:
www.libraryofalexandria.com

With gratitude and a shared love of knowledge,

The Modern Library of Alexandria Team

Visit:

www.libraryofalexandria.com

Or scan the code below:

Metaphysics

Aristotle's Ultimate Exploration of Reality, Existence, and Knowledge

A Modern Translation

Adapted for the Contemporary Reader

Aristotle

Translated by Tim Zengerink

Introduction

Ancient Greece was a civilization famous for its great contributions to philosophy, politics, art, and science. It thrived from the 8th century BCE until the Roman Empire started to decline. Greece's city-states, especially Athens, were the heart of culture and intellectual thought. This was the time when democracy began, impressive buildings like the Parthenon were built, and famous playwrights like Sophocles and Euripides produced their works. The Greeks' curiosity about the world around them laid the foundation for Western philosophy. Thinkers like Socrates, Plato, and later Aristotle, pushed the limits of what people understood about the world.

Greek society was deeply connected to theism, which focused on a large group of gods and goddesses who were believed to control every part of life. But this system did not prevent people from exploring new ideas. In fact, it coexisted with a growing interest in finding logical explanations for nature and human

life. Intellectuals would often debate and discuss these ideas in public places like the Agora. Aristotle grew up in this dynamic environment, learning from earlier philosophers, and later challenging and expanding their ideas.

Aristotle's Life

Aristotle was born in 384 BCE in a small town called Stagira, located in northern Greece. His father, Nicomachus, was a doctor for King Amyntas of Macedon, and this allowed Aristotle to be around the Macedonian royal court from a young age. When his parents passed away, Aristotle was sent to Athens at the age of 17 to pursue his education. Athens was the center of intellectual life in Greece, and Aristotle joined Plato's Academy, which was the most respected school of the time. The Academy was a place where students discussed everything from ethics to science. Although Aristotle learned a lot from Plato, he did not always agree with him, especially when it came to metaphysics, which deals with the nature of reality.

After spending almost 20 years at the Academy, Aristotle left Athens around 347 BCE after Plato's death. He traveled around different cities in Greece, continuing to study and learn. In 343 BCE, he was

invited to the court of King Philip II of Macedon, where he became the tutor of Philip's son, Alexander, who would later become known as Alexander the Great. Aristotle taught Alexander about philosophy, ethics, politics, and science. Aristotle's influence is visible in Alexander's leadership style, which showed respect for knowledge and strategic thinking.

After teaching Alexander, Aristotle returned to Athens in 335 BCE, where he opened his own school called the Lyceum. Unlike Plato's Academy, the Lyceum focused more on recording knowledge and observing nature. Aristotle and his students performed research, studied animals, and took notes on what they observed. The Lyceum became a major center of learning, and it rivaled Plato's Academy. This is also where Aristotle wrote many of his famous works.

Later in life, after the death of Alexander in 323 BCE, the political climate in Athens became difficult for Aristotle because of his connections to the Macedonian court. Accused of disrespecting the gods, Aristotle decided to leave Athens. He fled to Chalcis, where he passed away in 322 BCE. Even though he had to leave Athens, his legacy lived on through his many writings and the influence of his school, the Lyceum.

Aristotle's Impact on Western Thought

No figure looms larger over the development of Western philosophy and science than Aristotle. A student of Plato and tutor to Alexander the Great, he unified logic, ethics, politics, rhetoric, and metaphysics into a coherent system that shaped intellectual inquiry for centuries. Although his writings reflect the best knowledge of his era, they also reveal a distinctive way of understanding the world—one that balances observation with rigorous logical analysis. Over time, this method has profoundly influenced everything from political theory to modern scientific methodology.

Aristotle approached knowledge as an interconnected whole, seeing each field of study as a vital path toward truth. While many earlier thinkers focused on abstract concepts, he emphasized direct observation of the natural world. By systematically examining and classifying what he saw, Aristotle laid the groundwork for the empirical methods now central to modern science. Although our understanding of nature has evolved, his legacy endures in today's emphasis on evidence-based research.

Logic: The Foundation of Rational Inquiry

Often hailed as the "father of formal logic," Aristotle introduced a system of reasoning that shaped intellectual discourse for over two millennia. In works like the Organon, he analyzed how valid conclusions are drawn from premises and introduced syllogisms—deductive arguments that became standard tools in philosophy, theology, and science. Even contemporary logic, despite its modern mathematical and symbolic advancements, can trace many of its core principles back to Aristotle's pioneering analyses.

Metaphysics: Exploring the Nature of Reality

Aristotle's Metaphysics offered one of the earliest comprehensive explorations of existence at its most fundamental level. There, he described the nature of "being qua being" and introduced the concepts of potentiality and actuality to explain how things change and develop. These ideas deeply influenced medieval scholastics—both Christian and Islamic—who integrated Aristotelian reasoning into their theological frameworks. Today, discussions about consciousness, identity, and free will still reference these Aristotelian notions.

Ethics and the Pursuit of the Good Life

In the Nicomachean Ethics, Aristotle proposed that the ultimate aim of human life is eudaimonia, often translated as "happiness" or "flourishing." He argued that we achieve this through virtue, developed by cultivating good habits guided by reason. His famous Doctrine of the Mean asserts that moral virtue resides between two extremes—for instance, courage lies between recklessness and cowardice. This focus on character formation has profoundly shaped the tradition known as "virtue ethics," influencing modern debates on moral education, personal development, and what it means to live well.

Politics: The Role of the Individual in the City-State

Aristotle's practical approach to ethics naturally extended into political theory. In Politics, he explored various forms of government—monarchy, aristocracy, oligarchy, democracy—and weighed their merits and pitfalls. For Aristotle, a well-ordered polis (city-state) exists not merely for survival or trade but to enable its citizens to live virtuous, fulfilling lives. His conviction that ethics

and politics are intertwined remains influential, informing contemporary discussions on citizenship, governance, and justice.

Rhetoric: The Art of Persuasion

In his treatise Rhetoric, Aristotle examined how persuasion works, detailing how arguments must appeal to ethos (credibility), pathos (emotion), and logos (logic). This clear framework for effective communication continues to guide public speakers, legal advocates, and writers. From ancient courtroom orations to modern political campaigns, Aristotelian rhetoric underpins many of the strategies people use to sway audiences and shape public opinion.

Beyond these core subjects, Aristotle made significant contributions to biology, physics, psychology, and aesthetics. In the Poetics, for example, he investigated why humans respond so powerfully to tragic drama, pioneering the concept of catharsis—the emotional release that audiences feel through art. Throughout the medieval period, thinkers like Thomas Aquinas integrated Aristotle's theories into Christian theology, while Islamic philosophers such as Avicenna and Averroes preserved, interpreted, and expanded upon his works.

Across centuries of reinterpretation and debate, Aristotle remains a living voice in contemporary thought. His insistence on systematically gathering evidence and connecting it to logical principles laid the foundation for what we now recognize as the scientific method. His inquiries into human flourishing, civic responsibility, and the nature of argument continue to spark discussion and inspire new research. From personal ethics to societal organization, Aristotle's ideas help us frame enduring questions about how best to live, learn, and understand reality.

In sum, Aristotle stands as a foundational pillar of Western thought. He bridged abstract theorizing and practical inquiry, bequeathing a vision of knowledge that values both reason and experience. From ethics and politics to science and art, his ideas have been woven into countless intellectual traditions. Even today, as we grapple with questions of morality, governance, and truth, we walk in the footsteps of an ancient thinker whose breadth of insight and depth of analysis continue to guide our pursuit of wisdom.

Final Thoughts

By preserving Aristotle's legacy, we protect the intellectual depth and rigor that defined his way

of understanding the world. His systematic way of asking questions, his classification of knowledge, and his ethical theories are still relevant today, providing a model for critical thinking across many subjects. This preservation is important not just for philosophy students but for anyone interested in the foundations of human thought and the development of ideas that shape the world we live in.

One of the difficulties in studying Aristotle's work is that his ideas and language are complex. Translating these works into our modern language is a key step in making his profound insights easier for more people to understand. By putting his ideas into today's language, more readers can engage with his thoughts, even if they don't have a background in classical studies. Making Aristotle's work accessible means adapting them to modern ways of thinking without losing their original depth. This helps bridge the gap between ancient and modern readers, making sure Aristotle's work stays relevant.

Metaphysics

When it comes to predicting the future through dreams, we shouldn't quickly dismiss it as nonsense, but we also shouldn't fully trust it. The fact that many people believe dreams have special meanings makes us think there could be something to it, as it's based on real experiences. It's not impossible that some dreams could predict future events, which seems reasonable. This might make us believe that all dreams have some sort of meaning. However, the lack of any clear reason for this kind of prediction also makes us doubt it. For one thing, it seems strange to think that God would send dreams to predict the future but only to ordinary people, not to the wisest or best people. And if we take God out of the picture, none of the other explanations seem very likely either. How can it make sense that someone could dream about something happening far away, like at the ends of the Earth? Understanding that seems to go beyond what people are capable of.

So, we must think of these dreams as either causing events, being signs of events, or simply being coincidences. They could be all of these things, or just one of them. By "cause," I mean like how the moon causes a solar eclipse, or how being tired can cause a fever. By "sign," I mean like how the start of an eclipse shows it's happening, or how a rough tongue can be a sign of a fever. And by "coincidence," I mean like someone taking a walk during a solar eclipse—the walk doesn't cause the eclipse, and the eclipse doesn't cause the walk. That's why coincidences don't follow specific rules.

So, should we say that some dreams are causes and others are signs, like signs of things happening in the body? Doctors even say that we should pay attention to our dreams, and this makes sense for people who aren't doctors, too. Movements inside the body during the day are usually too small to notice because they are overshadowed by more obvious movements that happen while we are awake. But when we sleep, smaller movements seem bigger. This is clear from what often happens during sleep. For example, dreamers may think they hear thunder and lightning when it's just a faint ringing in their ears. Or they may think they're tasting honey or something sweet when it's only a little bit of phlegm in their throat. They might dream of walking through fire and feeling intense heat when it's just a slight warmth in part of their body. When they wake up, they realize what was really happening.

Since the beginnings of everything are small, this is also true for illnesses or other conditions about to affect the body. It's clear that these early signs are easier to notice when we are asleep than when we are awake.

It's also possible that some of the images that come to us in sleep can actually cause the actions related to them. When we are about to do something while awake or have just done something, we often dream about those actions. This happens because the movements of our dreams are connected to the movements we had during the day. In the same way, movements we experience in sleep could be the starting points for actions we take during the day. Our thoughts during the day may be linked to the images we saw during the night. So, it's possible that some dreams could be both signs and causes of future events.

Most dreams that are said to predict the future are just coincidences, especially those about strange things or events far away, like a sea battle, where the dreamer has no control over what happens. It's normal for people to sometimes mention something and then have it happen. So, why shouldn't this happen in dreams too? In fact, it's probably more likely to happen while we sleep. Just like saying someone's name doesn't cause them to show up, dreaming about something doesn't cause it to happen either—it's just a coincidence. This explains why many dreams don't come true, because coincidences don't follow specific rules.

Since even some animals dream, it's clear that dreams aren't sent by God to reveal the future. Dreams come from nature, which has a divine design, but nature itself isn't divine. One reason we know dreams aren't from God is that people who have vivid dreams or seem to predict the future often aren't the wisest or best people. This suggests that God isn't sending them dreams, but that some people who are more excitable or distracted just happen to have dreams that seem to predict real events. It's like playing a game of chance—if you guess enough times, you'll eventually guess correctly.

It's not surprising that many dreams don't come true, just like many weather predictions or signs of illness don't always turn out to be correct. For example, we might expect rain or wind based on certain signs, but if something else happens that's stronger, the rain or wind might not happen. In the same way, many things that people plan to do, no matter how well-planned, can be stopped by other, more powerful forces. Just because something was about to happen doesn't mean it will happen exactly as we expect. Still, we have to accept that the early signs of events are real, even if the event doesn't always follow.

As for dreams that don't seem to have natural signs and seem strange because of their timing, place, or scale, or when the dreamer has no control over the event, we shouldn't think of them as prophetic unless they're just coincidences. A better explanation than the one given by Democritus, who talked about "images" and "emanations," is this: When something causes movement in water or air, that movement continues even after the thing that caused it is gone. In the same way, a movement and a resulting perception can reach the mind during sleep, even if the cause is no longer there. This could explain how dreams can seem to predict the future, especially at night when the air is calm, and movements aren't disturbed like they are during the day when the air is more active. People are also more sensitive to small movements during sleep, which might explain why dreams seem to predict the future.

This could also explain why it's regular people, not the wisest ones, who seem to have prophetic dreams. If God were sending these dreams, they would happen during the day and to wise people. But since they don't, it makes sense that ordinary people have these dreams. These people don't spend much time thinking, so their minds are empty and easily moved by whatever comes along.

For people with mental illnesses, their normal thoughts don't get in the way of outside movements, which is why they seem to sense things more clearly. Some people have vivid dreams about people they know well because they are more concerned about those people. Just like friends can recognize each other from far away, they can also sense things about each other more easily in dreams. Familiar movements are easier to recognize. People with a lot of dark bile, who are more emotional, often "shoot from a distance" and hit the target, because their thoughts move quickly through their minds, just like people repeating lines from memory.

The best person to interpret dreams is someone who can see connections and similarities. Anyone can interpret clear and vivid dreams. By "seeing connections," I mean that dream images are like reflections in water, as we've said before. If the water is disturbed, the reflection looks nothing like the original image. A skilled interpreter can quickly recognize the scattered and distorted pieces of the reflection and see that they represent a person, a horse, or something else. In the same way, a dream is often like a blurry image, because the internal movements of the body make the dream unclear.

We've now discussed what sleep and dreams are, the causes behind them, and how dreams might be linked to predicting the future.

• • •

On Sense and the Sensible

Aristotle's Exploration of Perception and Reality

A Modern Translation

Adapted for the Contemporary Reader

Aristotle

Translated by Tim Zengerink

Introduction

Ancient Greece was a civilization famous for its great contributions to philosophy, politics, art, and science. It thrived from the 8th century BCE until the Roman Empire started to decline. Greece's city-states, especially Athens, were the heart of culture and intellectual thought. This was the time when democracy began, impressive buildings like the Parthenon were built, and famous playwrights like Sophocles and Euripides produced their works. The Greeks' curiosity about the world around them laid the foundation for Western philosophy. Thinkers like Socrates, Plato, and later Aristotle, pushed the limits of what people understood about the world.

Greek society was deeply connected to theism, which focused on a large group of gods and goddesses who were believed to control every part of life. But this system did not prevent people from exploring new ideas. In fact, it coexisted with a growing interest in finding logical explanations for nature and human

life. Intellectuals would often debate and discuss these ideas in public places like the Agora. Aristotle grew up in this dynamic environment, learning from earlier philosophers, and later challenging and expanding their ideas.

Aristotle's Life

Aristotle was born in 384 BCE in a small town called Stagira, located in northern Greece. His father, Nicomachus, was a doctor for King Amyntas of Macedon, and this allowed Aristotle to be around the Macedonian royal court from a young age. When his parents passed away, Aristotle was sent to Athens at the age of 17 to pursue his education. Athens was the center of intellectual life in Greece, and Aristotle joined Plato's Academy, which was the most respected school of the time. The Academy was a place where students discussed everything from ethics to science. Although Aristotle learned a lot from Plato, he did not always agree with him, especially when it came to metaphysics, which deals with the nature of reality.

After spending almost 20 years at the Academy, Aristotle left Athens around 347 BCE after Plato's death. He traveled around different cities in Greece, continuing to study and learn. In 343 BCE, he was

invited to the court of King Philip II of Macedon, where he became the tutor of Philip's son, Alexander, who would later become known as Alexander the Great. Aristotle taught Alexander about philosophy, ethics, politics, and science. Aristotle's influence is visible in Alexander's leadership style, which showed respect for knowledge and strategic thinking.

After teaching Alexander, Aristotle returned to Athens in 335 BCE, where he opened his own school called the Lyceum. Unlike Plato's Academy, the Lyceum focused more on recording knowledge and observing nature. Aristotle and his students performed research, studied animals, and took notes on what they observed. The Lyceum became a major center of learning, and it rivaled Plato's Academy. This is also where Aristotle wrote many of his famous works.

Later in life, after the death of Alexander in 323 BCE, the political climate in Athens became difficult for Aristotle because of his connections to the Macedonian court. Accused of disrespecting the gods, Aristotle decided to leave Athens. He fled to Chalcis, where he passed away in 322 BCE. Even though he had to leave Athens, his legacy lived on through his many writings and the influence of his school, the Lyceum.

Aristotle's Impact on Western Thought

No figure looms larger over the development of Western philosophy and science than Aristotle. A student of Plato and tutor to Alexander the Great, he unified logic, ethics, politics, rhetoric, and metaphysics into a coherent system that shaped intellectual inquiry for centuries. Although his writings reflect the best knowledge of his era, they also reveal a distinctive way of understanding the world—one that balances observation with rigorous logical analysis. Over time, this method has profoundly influenced everything from political theory to modern scientific methodology.

Aristotle approached knowledge as an interconnected whole, seeing each field of study as a vital path toward truth. While many earlier thinkers focused on abstract concepts, he emphasized direct observation of the natural world. By systematically examining and classifying what he saw, Aristotle laid the groundwork for the empirical methods now central to modern science. Although our understanding of nature has evolved, his legacy endures in today's emphasis on evidence-based research.

Logic: The Foundation of Rational Inquiry

Often hailed as the "father of formal logic," Aristotle introduced a system of reasoning that shaped intellectual discourse for over two millennia. In works like the Organon, he analyzed how valid conclusions are drawn from premises and introduced syllogisms—deductive arguments that became standard tools in philosophy, theology, and science. Even contemporary logic, despite its modern mathematical and symbolic advancements, can trace many of its core principles back to Aristotle's pioneering analyses.

Metaphysics: Exploring the Nature of Reality

Aristotle's Metaphysics offered one of the earliest comprehensive explorations of existence at its most fundamental level. There, he described the nature of "being qua being" and introduced the concepts of potentiality and actuality to explain how things change and develop. These ideas deeply influenced medieval scholastics—both Christian and Islamic—who integrated Aristotelian reasoning into their theological frameworks. Today, discussions about consciousness, identity, and free will still reference these Aristotelian notions.

Ethics and the Pursuit of the Good Life

In the Nicomachean Ethics, Aristotle proposed that the ultimate aim of human life is eudaimonia, often translated as "happiness" or "flourishing." He argued that we achieve this through virtue, developed by cultivating good habits guided by reason. His famous Doctrine of the Mean asserts that moral virtue resides between two extremes—for instance, courage lies between recklessness and cowardice. This focus on character formation has profoundly shaped the tradition known as "virtue ethics," influencing modern debates on moral education, personal development, and what it means to live well.

Politics: The Role of the Individual in the City-State

Aristotle's practical approach to ethics naturally extended into political theory. In Politics, he explored various forms of government—monarchy, aristocracy, oligarchy, democracy—and weighed their merits and pitfalls. For Aristotle, a well-ordered polis (city-state) exists not merely for survival or trade but to enable its citizens to live virtuous, fulfilling lives. His conviction that ethics

and politics are intertwined remains influential, informing contemporary discussions on citizenship, governance, and justice.

Rhetoric: The Art of Persuasion

In his treatise Rhetoric, Aristotle examined how persuasion works, detailing how arguments must appeal to ethos (credibility), pathos (emotion), and logos (logic). This clear framework for effective communication continues to guide public speakers, legal advocates, and writers. From ancient courtroom orations to modern political campaigns, Aristotelian rhetoric underpins many of the strategies people use to sway audiences and shape public opinion.

Beyond these core subjects, Aristotle made significant contributions to biology, physics, psychology, and aesthetics. In the Poetics, for example, he investigated why humans respond so powerfully to tragic drama, pioneering the concept of catharsis—the emotional release that audiences feel through art. Throughout the medieval period, thinkers like Thomas Aquinas integrated Aristotle's theories into Christian theology, while Islamic philosophers such as Avicenna and Averroes preserved, interpreted, and expanded upon his works.

Across centuries of reinterpretation and debate, Aristotle remains a living voice in contemporary thought. His insistence on systematically gathering evidence and connecting it to logical principles laid the foundation for what we now recognize as the scientific method. His inquiries into human flourishing, civic responsibility, and the nature of argument continue to spark discussion and inspire new research. From personal ethics to societal organization, Aristotle's ideas help us frame enduring questions about how best to live, learn, and understand reality.

In sum, Aristotle stands as a foundational pillar of Western thought. He bridged abstract theorizing and practical inquiry, bequeathing a vision of knowledge that values both reason and experience. From ethics and politics to science and art, his ideas have been woven into countless intellectual traditions. Even today, as we grapple with questions of morality, governance, and truth, we walk in the footsteps of an ancient thinker whose breadth of insight and depth of analysis continue to guide our pursuit of wisdom.

Final Thoughts

By preserving Aristotle's legacy, we protect the intellectual depth and rigor that defined his way

of understanding the world. His systematic way of asking questions, his classification of knowledge, and his ethical theories are still relevant today, providing a model for critical thinking across many subjects. This preservation is important not just for philosophy students but for anyone interested in the foundations of human thought and the development of ideas that shape the world we live in.

One of the difficulties in studying Aristotle's work is that his ideas and language are complex. Translating these works into our modern language is a key step in making his profound insights easier for more people to understand. By putting his ideas into today's language, more readers can engage with his thoughts, even if they don't have a background in classical studies. Making Aristotle's work accessible means adapting them to modern ways of thinking without losing their original depth. This helps bridge the gap between ancient and modern readers, making sure Aristotle's work stays relevant.

Section 1

Now that we have fully considered the soul and its different abilities, the next step is to look at animals and all living things to understand which abilities are unique to them and which are shared. What we've already determined about the soul on its own will apply here too. Now, we need to address the remaining aspects that involve both the soul and the body, starting with the most basic ones.

The most important traits of animals, whether shared by all or unique to some, are clearly those of both the soul and body together, like sensation, memory, emotions, desires, and pleasure and pain. These traits can be said to belong to all animals. However, beyond these, there are some traits shared by all living things, while others are unique to certain types of animals. The most important of these traits can be grouped into four pairs: being awake and asleep, youth and old age, breathing in and out, and life and death. We must try to understand these scientifically, figuring out what they are and why they happen.

The philosopher who studies nature must also understand the basics of health and disease because neither of these can exist in things that aren't alive. In fact, we can say that most physical researchers and doctors who study medicine philosophically complete their work with discussions on health, while doctors often base their medical ideas on principles learned from nature.

It's obvious that all the traits listed above belong to both the soul and body working together because they all involve sensation in some way or depend on it. Some are feelings or states related to sensation, others protect and preserve it, and some cause its loss or absence. It's clear from both reasoning and observation that sensation occurs in the soul through the body.

In our work on the soul, we already explained the nature of sensation, how we perceive through it, and why this ability belongs to animals. Sensation must indeed be attributed to all animals because its presence or absence is what separates animals from non-animals.

Now, looking at each sense individually, we can say that touch and taste are necessary for all animals. Touch is essential for the reasons we explained in the work on the soul, and taste is needed for nutrition. It's through taste that animals distinguish between pleasant and unpleasant foods, so they can avoid the bad and go after the good. In general, flavor is a quality of nourishing substances.

The senses that work through external media—smell, hearing, and sight—are found in all animals that can move. For all animals that have these senses, they serve as tools for survival, allowing them to seek food and avoid harmful or dangerous things based on prior sensations. But for animals that also possess intelligence, these senses help them reach higher levels of understanding. They provide information about many different qualities of things, leading to knowledge of truth, both theoretical and practical, in the soul.

Of the last two senses mentioned, sight is more important for basic survival needs, but hearing is more important for developing intelligence. Sight, because all bodies have color, provides information about many different characteristics of things, allowing us to perceive common qualities like shape, size, movement, and number. Hearing, on the other hand, only tells us about the unique qualities of sound and, for a few animals, voice. However, indirectly, hearing contributes more to the growth of intelligence. This is because speech, which teaches us things, is heard. Speech is made up of words, and each word represents a thought. Therefore, among people who are born without either sense, those who are blind are generally more intelligent than those who are deaf and mute.

We've already discussed the unique abilities of each of the senses.

Now, let's consider the nature of the sense organs, or the parts of the body where each sense is naturally found. Many researchers base their ideas on the basic elements that make up everything. But they struggle to match five senses with just four elements, which confuses them about the fifth sense. For example, they believe that the organ of sight is made of fire because when the eye is pressed or moved, it seems like fire flashes from it. This happens most clearly in the dark or when the eyelids are closed, because darkness is produced then too.

But this idea only solves one problem while creating another. Unless we assume that someone can see an object without realizing it, this theory would mean that the eye sees itself. But why doesn't this "flash" happen when the eye is still? The true explanation for this can be found in understanding how smooth things naturally shine in the dark, without giving off light. The black part of the eye, its center, is smooth. The flash only happens when the eye moves quickly because this movement makes one object appear to be two. The speed of the motion makes what is seen and what is seeing seem like two different things. This doesn't happen unless the motion is fast and in the dark. It's in the dark that smooth things, like the heads of certain fish, naturally shine. If the eye moves slowly, the same object can't appear to be two at once. In reality, the eye sees itself in this flash the same way it does when reflected in a mirror.

If the organ for sight really was made of fire, as Empedocles believed, and as it's suggested in the Timaeus, and if sight was caused by light coming from the eye like from a lantern, why can't the eye see in the dark? It's pointless to say, like in the Timaeus, that the visual ray is "quenched" in the dark. What does it mean for light to be "quenched"? Something hot and dry, like burning coals or fire, can be quenched by something cold or wet. But light doesn't seem to have heat or dryness. Or if it does, and it's just so slight we can't notice, we should expect the sun's light to be quenched during rain or in freezing weather. Flames and burning objects can be put out this way, but sunlight is not.

Empedocles sometimes explains vision by light coming from the eye, like in this passage:

"Like someone preparing a lantern

To shine in the stormy night,

Setting clear sides around the fire

To protect it from the wind,

While the fire leaps out and shines

Its constant beams over the threshold."

Here, he explains vision by fire within the eye, but at other times, he says vision comes from things outside the eye.

Democritus, on the other hand, correctly says the eye is made of water. However, he is wrong when he explains sight as just reflecting images like a mirror. The reflection happens because the eye is smooth, and the reflection occurs not in the eye that is seen, but in the one that sees. It's just a case of reflection. But even in his time, there wasn't enough knowledge about how images and reflections form. It's strange that he didn't ask why, if his theory is true, the eye is the only thing that sees, while other reflective surfaces do not.

It's true that the eye is made of water, but it sees not because of that, but because it is translucent, which is a quality shared by both water and air. However, water is easier to contain and condense than air, which is why the eye is made of water. This is proven by actual experience. When eyes decompose, the liquid that comes out is water, and in embryos, this liquid is cold and shiny. In animals with blood, the white part of the eye is oily and fatty to prevent the moisture from freezing. This is why the eye doesn't feel cold; no one feels cold in the area protected by the eyelids. Bloodless animals have eyes protected by a hard scale, which serves the same purpose.

Overall, it doesn't make sense to say the eye sees because something comes out of it. The idea that light from the eye stretches all the way to the stars, or only to a certain point before joining rays from the object, is unreasonable. If this were true, the merging of rays would happen inside the eye itself. But even this is just speculation. What does it mean for light to "merge" with other light? How could the light inside the eye merge with the light outside it, when the membrane around the eye is in between?

We've said before that sight is impossible without light, but whether the medium is air or light, vision happens through that medium.

Therefore, it's easy to understand that the inner part of the eye is made of water, because water is translucent.

Just as vision is impossible without light outside the eye, it's also impossible without light inside the eye. There must be something translucent inside the eye, and since it's not air, it must be water. The soul, or the part of it that perceives, isn't on the surface of the eye but somewhere inside. That's why the inside of the eye must be capable of letting in light. We know this is true from real experiences. When soldiers are wounded in battle by a sword that cuts through the eye's passages, they suddenly feel darkness, as if a lamp went out. This is because the pupil, the translucent part that acts like an inner lamp, is cut off from the soul.

So, if all these facts are correct, it's clear that if we explain the sense organs by matching them with the four elements, we should say the part of the eye involved in vision is made of water, the part involved in hearing is made of air, and the sense of smell is related to fire. (I'm talking about the sense of smell, not the organ itself.) The organ of smell is only potentially what the sense of smell becomes when it is activated by its object. Smell is like a smoky vapor, and smoke comes from fire. This helps explain why the olfactory organ is near the brain, as cold matter has the potential to become hot. The same reasoning applies to the development of the eye. Its structure comes from the brain, which is the wettest and coldest part of the body.

The organ of touch is made of earth, and taste is a specific kind of touch. This explains why both touch and taste are closely connected to the heart, since the heart, being the hottest part of the body, balances the coldness of the brain.

This is how we should understand the characteristics of the sense organs.

We have already discussed the qualities connected to each of the senses, like color, sound, smell, taste, and touch, in On the Soul. There, we talked about their purpose and how they become actual through their respective sense organs. Now, we must explain each of them in more detail—what we mean by color, sound, smell, taste, and touch. Let's start with color.

Each of these can be thought of in two ways: as potential or as actual. In On the Soul, we explained how the actualized version of color or sound is similar to and different from the act of seeing or hearing. The goal of this discussion is to figure out what each sensory quality must be in itself in order for it to be perceived.

We already said in On the Soul that light is the color of the translucent, and this happens when a fiery element is present in a clear medium. When the fiery element is not present, the result is darkness. However, translucence itself isn't something unique to air, water, or any other clear substances; it's a quality that can be found in all bodies to some degree. Translucence doesn't exist by itself but is present within these substances. Since every body with translucence has an outer boundary, translucence must also have one. So, we can say that light is the nature of the translucent when it is not limited by any boundaries. However, when translucence exists within a bounded body, its boundary must be something real. This is where color comes in—color is found at the outer limit of the body, either as part of the body's surface or as the surface itself. This is why the Pythagoreans called the surface of a body its "hue," because hue lies at the boundary of a body. But the boundary isn't a separate thing; we can imagine that the same substance that carries color on the outside also exists inside the body.

Even air and water seem to have color because they are bright, which is similar to having color. But the color of air or the sea is different depending on how far away you are from it. When you get closer, the color changes. In solid objects, the color is fixed unless the surrounding atmosphere changes it. This shows that the thing that allows color to exist is the same in both cases. So, it's the translucence in bodies that causes them to take on color, depending on how much translucence they have. Since color exists at the boundary of the body, it must also exist at the boundary of the translucent part within the body. Therefore, we can define color as the limit of translucence in a solid body. Whether we are talking about translucent things like water or solid things with fixed colors, they all show their colors at their outer surfaces.

The same thing that produces light in air can also be present in the translucence inside solid bodies, or it might not be present, resulting in the absence of light. Just like how air can have light or darkness, solid objects can have the colors white or black.

Now, let's talk about the other colors and go over the different ideas people have come up with to explain how they are created.

1. It's possible that white and black are mixed together in such tiny amounts that neither one is visible on its own, but the combination of both creates a new color. This new color wouldn't be white or black but something different. This could explain how we get a variety of colors besides white and black. These colors could also be produced by

different ratios of black to white. For example, the ratio could be 3 to 2 or 3 to 4, creating different colors, while other colors might not follow any specific ratio. Some of these colors might be like the notes in music, where certain ratios are more pleasing, such as purple, crimson, and a few others. These colors are rare for the same reason that musical harmonies are few in number. Other colors might come from irregular combinations of black and white. Some colors could be based on precise ratios, while others might be irregular, leading to impure colors due to the way the ratio is arranged. This is one possible explanation for how we get different colors.

2. Another idea is that black and white appear through each other, creating an effect like what happens when painters layer one color on top of another to make an object look like it's underwater or in a fog. The same thing happens when the sun, which is naturally white, looks red when seen through a fog or smoke. According to this idea, different colors could also arise from this mixing, depending on the ratio of the top color to the bottom color. But it doesn't make sense to say, like some ancient thinkers did, that colors come from objects emitting something. They would still have to explain how sense perception happens through touch, so it's

better to say that perception happens because the object affects the medium between it and the sense organ.

If we accept the idea of colors being side by side, we also have to assume that both the size of the colors and the time they take to appear are so small that we don't notice them. This way, the combination of colors appears as one. But if we follow the idea of one color being on top of another, we don't need to make this assumption. The effect that the top color has on the medium will change depending on whether it is affected by the color underneath it. So, the result will be a color that is neither white nor black. If we can't assume that any size can be invisible, and we have to believe that everything is visible from some distance, then this second idea of colors being layered can also be seen as a valid theory of color mixing.

3. There is also a third idea, which says that bodies don't just mix by putting their smallest parts side by side, but that their material is fully combined together. We discussed this in the treatise on Mixture. This kind of mixing, where the material is blended together, is the most complete form of mixture. When bodies mix this way, their colors are mixed too, and this is what causes there to be many colors. When bodies mix, the color looks the same from

any distance, unlike when colors are just layered or placed side by side, where the color changes depending on how close you are.

Colors will still be many in number because the materials can combine in many different ratios. Some colors will come from specific ratios of materials, while others will result from irregular amounts. Everything we said about colors being side by side or layered also applies to this kind of mixing.

We will discuss later why colors, tastes, and sounds exist in specific types instead of being infinite in number.

We have now explained what color is and why there are many colors. Before this, in our work On the Soul, we explained the nature of sound and voice. Now, we need to discuss smell and taste. These two are almost the same in how they affect us physically, though they come from different sources. Tastes are easier for us to understand than smells because the sense of smell in humans is weaker than in animals. Among our senses, smell is the least perfect, while our sense of touch is the finest, and taste is a part of touch.

Water, by itself, doesn't have much taste. But since we can't taste without water, we have to think about how water works with taste. Either (a) we can say that water already has tiny, invisible amounts of all different tastes mixed in it, as Empedocles believed; or (b) water is like a base that can develop different tastes from different parts of itself; or (c) water doesn't have any taste on its own, but something else, like heat or the sun, causes it to have taste.

(a) It's easy to see that Empedocles' idea is wrong. When fruits are picked and left in the sun or put near fire, their juices change because of the heat. This shows that the change doesn't come from the water they got from the ground, but from something happening inside the fruit. We also see that juices, when left out, change from sweet to bitter or other tastes over time. Boiling or fermenting these juices can also give them new tastes.

(b) It's also impossible that water is made in a way that different parts of it can produce different tastes, because we see different tastes come from the same water, which is used to nourish them.

(c) The only option left is to think that water changes by receiving some effect from something else. It's clear that water doesn't get its taste just from heat. Water is thinner than any other liquid, even oil. Although oil is thicker and stickier, it's easier to handle than water because water doesn't hold together. Since pure water doesn't become thick when heated, we have to think that something besides heat causes taste. All things with taste have some level of thickness. Heat helps in this process, but it isn't the only cause.

The juices in fruits come from the earth. That's why some of the older philosophers said that water takes on the qualities of the earth it flows through. This is especially clear with salty water from springs, because salt is a type of earth. Also, when liquids are filtered through ashes, they become bitter. Some wells have bitter water, some are acidic, and others have different kinds of tastes.

As we might expect, the plant world has the most variety of tastes. In nature, moist things are affected by their opposite, which is dryness. That's why moist things are affected by fire, which is naturally dry. Heat is the main property of fire, just as dryness is the main property of earth. So fire and earth, by themselves, can't affect each other directly. In fact, no two natural things can affect each other unless there is some kind of opposite quality between them.

Just like people can wash colors or tastes into water, nature does the same thing. It washes the dry and earthy things in moisture and filters it. This happens when heat moves through the dry and earthy parts, giving the water a certain quality. This change, caused by the dry part acting on the moist, makes it possible for us to taste. Taste takes what was just a potential ability to sense and makes it an actual experience. This is similar to how our other senses work, not by learning something new, but by using what we already know.

Tastes belong to food that can nourish us, and this becomes clearer when we realize that neither dry things without moisture nor moist things without dryness can nourish. Only things made from a mix of both can feed animals. The tangible parts of food, like whether it is hot or cold, are what cause animals to grow or decay. Heat or coldness directly causes growth or decay. But it's the taste of food that gives nourishment. All living things are nourished by sweetness, either by itself or mixed with other tastes. We will discuss this more in our work on Generation, but for now, we only need to mention what is necessary for this discussion. Heat causes growth and helps the food become digestible. It pulls in the light things, like sweetness, and rejects the heavy things, like salt and bitterness. The heat inside living things works the same way the heat outside of them does. This is how nourishment comes from sweetness. Other tastes are added to food in the same way we season food with salt or acid to balance out the sweetness. These tastes stop the sweet food from being too rich and light for the stomach.

Just like mixing white and black gives us in-between colors, mixing sweet and bitter gives us in-between tastes. These mixed tastes either have a specific balance or an undefined mixture of the two. Some tastes are mixed in exact amounts, which affects how they stimulate us, while others are mixed in ways that can't be exactly measured. Tastes that are pleasing come from a balance in their mixture.

The sweet taste is rich, and rich can be seen as a kind of sweet. On the other hand, salty is very similar to bitter, since both lack sweetness. Between sweet and bitter are harsh, pungent, astringent, and sour tastes. There are about as many different kinds of tastes as there are colors. We can say there are seven main kinds of each. For example, we could consider gray as a kind of black, or we could group yellow with white, just as rich goes with sweet. The basic colors like crimson, violet, leek-green, and deep blue are between white and black, and all other colors come from mixing these.

Just as black is the absence of white in something transparent, bitter or salty is the absence of sweetness in food. This is why ashes of burned things are bitter, because the sweet moisture has been burned away.

Democritus and other natural philosophers who study sense-perception are wrong because they treat everything we sense as a kind of touch. If that were true, it would mean all of our senses are really just touch, but that doesn't make sense.

They also treat things that all senses can perceive as if only one sense can perceive them. Qualities like size, shape, roughness, and smoothness are things that can be sensed by sight and touch, and this is why we can sometimes make mistakes about them. But when it comes to things that only one sense can perceive, like color or sound, there is no confusion.

They also confuse things that are specific to one sense with things that all senses can perceive, like when Democritus says white and black are just different kinds of rough and smooth. He also says taste comes from atomic shapes. But it's clear that no one sense, or if any, it would be sight, is better at perceiving common qualities. If taste were better at this, it would mean taste could sense shapes better than anything else.

All the things we sense have opposites. For example, white is the opposite of black, and sweet is the opposite of bitter. But no shape is the opposite of another shape. So, which polygon shape that Democritus says is bitter is the opposite of the spherical shape he says is sweet?

Since there are an infinite number of shapes, there should also be an infinite number of tastes. But if that were true, why would we be able to sense some tastes and not others?

This finishes our discussion of taste. The other effects of taste will be talked about more in our study of plants.

•••

Section 2

Our understanding of smells must be similar to how we understand tastes. Just like how dry things with taste affect both air and water but in different ways, the dry things that cause smell affect air and water too, but through different senses. We usually say that both air and water are transparent, but they don't carry smells because they are transparent. Instead, they carry smells because they can wash and absorb the dry substances that create smells.

Smell exists not just in the air but also in water. We know this because fish and shellfish can smell, even though water doesn't have air in it (because any air in water rises to the surface), and these animals don't breathe. So, if we assume that both air and water are moist, then smell is a natural substance made of dry things that have taste, spread out in the moisture, and anything like that would be something we can smell.

We can see that the ability to smell is based on something having taste by comparing things that have smell to things that don't. The basic elements, like fire, air, earth, and water, don't have smells because the dry and moist parts of them don't have taste unless something is added to give them taste. This explains why seawater has a smell—because, unlike pure water, it has both taste and dryness. Salt also has more smell than natron, as we can see from the oil that comes from salt. Natron is more similar to pure earth than salt is. A stone doesn't have a smell because it has no taste, but wood has a smell because it does have taste. Different types of wood that have more water in them smell less than others. If we look at metals, gold has no smell because it has no taste, but bronze and iron do have smells. When the moisture with taste burns out of these metals, the leftover slag has less smell than the metals themselves. Silver and tin smell more than some metals, but less than others, because they contain more water than some but less than others.

Some people think that smell comes from fumid exhalation, which is a mix of earth and air. Heraclitus seemed to believe this when he said that if everything turned into smoke, we would use our noses to sense them. Many people believe that smell comes from some kind of exhalation. Some think it comes from water, others think it comes from smoke, and others believe it comes from either one. Aqueous exhalation is just a form of moisture, but fumid exhalation is a mix of air and earth. When the first type condenses, it turns into water. The second type turns into a specific kind of earth. But it's unlikely that smell comes from either of these. Vaporous exhalation is just water, and since water has no taste, it has no smell. And fumid exhalation can't happen in water, but, as we've already said, creatures in water also have the ability to smell.

Also, the idea that smell comes from exhalation is similar to the idea that it comes from emanations. If the emanation theory isn't correct, then the exhalation theory probably isn't either.

It makes sense that moist things, whether in air or water (since air is also naturally moist), can absorb the effects of dry things that have taste. If the dry things in moist places like air and water create an effect as if they have been washed, then smells must be something like tastes. In fact, this is true in some cases, because we use the same words to describe both smells and tastes. For example, we say that smells and tastes can be pungent, sweet, harsh, astringent, or rich. We can even think of bad smells like we think of bitter tastes. This is why bad smells are unpleasant to breathe in, just like bitter tastes are unpleasant to swallow. So, it's clear that smell in both water and air works in a similar way to taste, which only happens in water. This also explains why cold and freezing make tastes dull and completely get rid of smells, because cold stops the heat that helps create taste.

There are two types of smells. Some writers say that smells can't be divided into types, but this isn't true. We need to explain how these two types can be recognized.

One kind of smell is like tastes. Whether these smells are pleasant or unpleasant depends on other factors. Since tastes are qualities of food, the smells related to them are nice when animals are hungry for the food, but not nice when they are full and don't want the food anymore. These smells aren't pleasant to animals that don't like the food the smell comes from. So, as we said, these smells are pleasant or unpleasant based on the situation, and this is why all animals can sense these smells.

The other kind of smell is the kind that is pleasant by its very nature, like the smell of flowers. These smells don't make animals want food and don't create appetite; in fact, they might even have the opposite effect. As the poet Strattis joked about Euripides: "Don't use perfume to flavor soup." This shows a truth—perfume doesn't belong in food.

People who add perfumes to drinks these days are teaching us to mix different sensations of pleasure, so we start to enjoy a mix of things that should feel separate.

Humans are the only ones who can sense this second type of smell. The first kind, the one connected to taste, can be sensed by all animals. Since the pleasantness of these smells depends on taste, they can be divided into as many types as there are tastes. But we can't say the same for the other type of smell, the one that is pleasant or unpleasant on its own. The reason humans are the only ones who can sense this type of smell is connected to the way our brains are. The human brain is naturally cold, and the blood in it is thin and pure but cools easily (this is why food smells, when cooled by the brain's coldness, can cause unhealthy effects like runny noses). So, these kinds of smells are made for human health. That is their only purpose, and it's clear that they do this job. Food, whether dry or moist, might taste sweet but still be unhealthy, while a pleasant smell is almost always good for our health.

For this reason, the sense of smell works through breathing in, but this only happens in humans and some other animals with blood, like four-legged animals and those that breathe air. When smells, which have heat in them, rise to the brain, they help the health of this part of the body. Smells naturally give warmth. This is why nature uses breathing for two things: first, to help the chest, and second, to let in smells. When an animal breathes in, the smell comes in through the nose, almost like sneaking in through a side entrance.

The second type of smell we talked about is only sensed by humans, and not by all animals. This is because humans have larger, moister brains than any other animals compared to their body size. This is also why humans are the only animals who seem to enjoy the smell of flowers and similar things. The warmth and stimulation caused by these smells match the coldness and moisture in the human brain. For other animals with lungs, nature gave them the ability to sense one of the two types of smell (the one related to food) when they breathe, so they don't need two different organs to sense smell. For these animals, breathing gives them the ability to sense the type of smell they need, just like humans can sense both kinds of smell through breathing.

It's clear that animals that don't breathe can still smell. Fish and insects, for example, have a strong sense of smell for finding their food, even from far away. Bees and small ants, like those called knipes, can smell their food from a distance. Marine animals like the murex and other similar creatures can also smell their food clearly.

It's not always clear which organ they use to smell. This question of how they smell can be tricky if we think that smelling only happens when animals breathe. It's clear that animals that breathe only smell while breathing, but the animals we just talked about don't breathe and still smell things—unless they have some unknown sense. But that's impossible. Any sense that detects smell is a sense of smell, and these animals clearly do smell, though they probably don't do it in the same way as animals that breathe. For animals that breathe, the act of breathing removes something that covers the organ of smell (this explains why they can't smell when they're not breathing). For animals that don't breathe, this covering is never there, just like how some animals have eyelids that block their vision when closed, while animals without eyelids can see all the time.

Based on what we've said, no lower animals avoid things that smell bad unless the bad smell is actually harmful. They can still be harmed by these smells, just like humans can. Humans can get headaches or even die from strong fumes like those from charcoal. Similarly, lower animals are killed by the strong smells of things like sulfur or bitumen. This is why they avoid these smells, not because they dislike them but because they have learned from experience that the smells are dangerous. They don't care about unpleasant smells unless those smells change the taste of their food.

Since we have an odd number of senses, and an odd number always has a middle point, smell is in the middle between touch (which includes taste) and the senses that work through a medium (like sight and hearing). This means that the things we smell are connected to both food (which is a tangible thing) and to things that can be heard or seen. This is why creatures can smell both in air and in water. So, smell belongs to both these worlds, connected to both things we touch and things that are heard or seen. This is why we describe smell as something dry that gets washed in something moist and fluid. That's how we should understand when it makes sense to say that smells have different types.

The idea some Pythagoreans had, that some animals live off smells alone, is incorrect. First, we see that food has to be a mix of things because the bodies it feeds are not simple. This is why waste is produced from food, either inside the body or, like in plants, outside of it. Even water on its own can't be food because something that can nourish must have a solid form. It's even harder to imagine that air could become solid enough to be food. Also, all animals have a place in their bodies to store food, from which the body absorbs it. The organ for smelling is in the head, and smells enter with the breath, going to the lungs. So it's clear that smell, by itself, doesn't give nutrition. But it's also clear that smell is good for health, as we can sense directly and as we've already discussed. Smell is to general health what taste is to nutrition and the body.

This concludes our discussion of the senses and how we perceive them.

One might ask: if every physical object can be divided into smaller and smaller parts forever, can the things we sense, like color, taste, smell, sound, weight, cold, heat, heaviness, lightness, hardness, or softness, also be divided forever? Or is this impossible?

This is a good question because each of these qualities is something we can sense, and they all get their name because they can affect our senses. So, if this is true, our ability to sense them should also be able to divide forever, and every tiny part of a body, no matter how small, should still be something we can sense. For example, it's impossible to see something that is white without it being a certain size.

If the qualities of a body couldn't be divided just like the body itself, we could imagine a body that exists without color, weight, or any other quality like that. This would mean that the body wouldn't be something we can sense at all because those qualities are what we sense. If that were true, then every object we can sense would be made of parts that we can't actually sense. But that can't be the case because objects aren't made of abstract or mathematical parts that don't exist in reality. Also, how would we be able to recognize these hypothetical real things without any qualities? Would we use reason? But reason doesn't deal with physical objects unless it works with our senses.

If this idea were true, it would support the idea of atoms. This could solve the question we started with, but the atom theory is impossible. We've already explained our views on atoms in our work on Movement.

Solving these questions will also explain why the kinds of color, taste, sound, and other qualities are limited. For everything that lies between two extremes has to be limited. Opposites are extremes, and everything we sense has an opposite. For example, in color, white and black are opposites. In taste, sweet and bitter are opposites, and all other senses have opposites as well. Something that is continuous can be divided into an infinite number of unequal parts but only into a limited number of equal parts. Things that are not continuous can only be divided into a certain number of species. Since the things we sense are divided into species, and they are continuous, we have to understand the difference between potential and actual.

This difference explains why we don't see every tiny part of a grain of millet, even though we can see the whole grain. It also explains why we don't notice the sound within a small musical interval, like a quarter-tone, even though we hear the whole song. The extremely small parts of things we sense go unnoticed because they are only potentially, but not actually, visible unless they are separated from the whole. Just like how a foot-length exists potentially within two feet, it only becomes real when it is separated from the whole. But if these tiny parts are separated from the whole, they could disappear into their surroundings, like a drop of flavored liquid dissolving in the sea. Even if that doesn't happen, since the sense-perception itself isn't something that can be sensed by itself or exist separately, we can't sense its tiny objects when they are separated from the whole. But even though these tiny parts are hard to perceive, they are still considered potentially perceptible and will become actually perceptible when they are part of a larger whole.

So, we have shown that some magnitudes and their qualities escape our notice and explained why this happens and how they are still sensed or not sensed. When these tiny parts of things we sense come together in a whole in a way that we can sense them again, not just because they are part of the whole but even when they are separate from it, their qualities, like color, taste, or sound, are limited in number.

One might also ask: do the things we sense, or the movements that come from them (whether we sense them by something being emitted or through some kind of motion), always first reach a middle point between the sense organ and the object, like smells and sounds do? For example, someone who is closer to the source of a smell will notice it before someone farther away, and we hear the sound of a hit after it has already happened. Is this also true for things we see and for light? Empedocles, for instance, says that the light from the sun first reaches the space between us before it reaches the earth or our eyes. This could seem reasonable because anything that moves through space has to travel from one place to another, and that would take time. But since any amount of time can be divided into parts, we would have to assume there is a time when the sun's rays hadn't yet reached us and were still traveling through the space in between.

Now, even if it's true that the act of hearing or seeing happens all at once and doesn't involve a process of becoming, just like how the sound from a hit has already happened before it reaches our ears, we still know that the sound takes time to travel through space. We can prove this because we sometimes hear words from a distance in a distorted way, which shows that sound is moving through space. So, the question is: does the same thing happen with color and light? We don't see something just because there is a general relationship between us and the object, like two things being equal to each other. If that were true, it wouldn't matter how close or far the object is.

It makes sense that this happens with sound and smell because they, like air and water, are continuous, but their movement can be divided into parts. This is why the person closest to the sound or smell perceives the same thing as the person farther away, but the farther person perceives it later.

Some people question this and say it's impossible for two people in different places to hear, see, or smell the same thing. They argue that the same thing can't be divided between them. But the answer is that everyone senses the same original object, like a bell, some incense, or fire. But each person's perception of the object is numerically different, even though it is the same type of thing. This is how many people can see, smell, or hear the same object at the same time. These things, like smells and sounds, are not bodies but are processes or effects of something. If they were bodies, then it wouldn't be possible for multiple people to sense them at once. But they do depend on a body to exist.

However, light is different. Light exists because something is there, not because of movement. In fact, qualitative change, like color, is different from movement in space. When something moves from one place to another, it has to pass through a middle point first (and sound is thought to be the movement of something through space), but we can't say the same about changes in qualities. These kinds of changes can happen all at once. For example, it's possible that water could freeze everywhere at the same time. But even in these cases, if the body being heated or cooled is large, each part of it changes in sequence, with the part next to it changing first. The part that changes first is changed by the source of the change, but the change throughout the whole body doesn't happen all at once. Tasting would be like smelling if we lived in a liquid environment and could sense flavors from a distance before touching the food.

Naturally, the parts of the space between a sense organ and its object don't all get affected at the same time, except in the case of light and sight, for the reasons we just discussed. Light causes us to see.

Another question about sense-perception is this: if it is natural that when two sensory inputs happen at the same time, the stronger one always pushes out the weaker one from our awareness, can we still perceive two things at the same time? This idea explains why people don't notice things in front of them when they are deep in thought, scared, or listening to a loud noise. We should accept this idea and also another one: it is easier to sense something in its pure form than when it is mixed with something else. For example, it is easier to taste wine by itself than when it is mixed with something, or to taste honey in its pure form. The same goes for color or hearing a musical note by itself rather than together with other notes. The reason is that when things are mixed, they tend to cancel out some of each other's characteristics. This happens whenever different things are mixed to form something new.

If the stronger input tends to push out the weaker one, it also means that when they happen together, the stronger one will be less noticeable than it would be by itself. This is because the weaker one blends with it and takes away some of its uniqueness, based on the idea that simple things are always easier to sense clearly.

Now, if two inputs are equally strong but different from each other, you won't be able to sense either one clearly. They will cancel each other out. If this happens, you won't be able to sense either one in its pure form. So, either you won't sense anything at all, or you will sense a mixture of both, which will be different from either one alone. This is what seems to happen when things are mixed, no matter what kind of mixture it is.

Since a mixture is created from some things that happen together, but not from others, and since things that belong to different senses don't mix (for example, you can't mix white and sharp, except in an indirect way, like how harmony is made from high and low notes), it follows that it's impossible to sense two different things at the same time. We have to assume that when two inputs are equal, they cancel each other out because they don't combine into one thing. But if one is stronger, only that one will be sensed clearly.

It's also more likely that the soul would sense two things at the same time when they are from the same sense, like low and high sounds. It's easier for inputs from the same sense to happen at the same time than inputs from two different senses, like sight and hearing. But it's impossible to sense two things at the same time with the same sense unless they are mixed together because once they mix, they become one. And when the object is one, the act of sensing it is also one, and the act of sensing something one is naturally happening all at once. So, when things are mixed, we have to sense them at the same time because we sense them as one. When something is one thing, we sense it with one perception. But when things haven't been mixed, we have two separate perceptions, which means we sense them one after the other, not at the same time. This is because the sense faculty can only have one act of perception at any moment, and since the sense organ is one, it can only focus on one thing at a time. This means that it's not possible to sense two different things at the same time with the same sense.

If it's impossible to sense two different things at the same time with the same sense, it's even less possible to sense things from two different senses, like white and sweet, at the same time. It seems that when the soul perceives something as one, it's because it senses it at the same time with one act of perception. But when it perceives two different things, it recognizes them as two because they are sensed in different ways. For example, the same sense can perceive white and black because they are part of the same type of perception, even though they are different from each other. Another sense, like taste, can perceive sweet and bitter. Both of these senses perceive things in their own ways, but the way they work is similar. For example, taste perceives sweet in the same way sight perceives white. And just like sight perceives black, taste perceives bitter.

If inputs from opposites are themselves opposites, and opposites can't exist together in the same subject, and if opposites like sweet and bitter are perceived by the same sense, then it's impossible to sense them at the same time. It's also impossible to sense things from the same sense that are not opposites but still different from each other. For example, in colors, some are grouped with white, and others with black. The same goes for tastes; some are grouped with sweet, and others with bitter. You can't sense the parts of mixtures at the same time (for example, the octave or the fifth in music, which are ratios of opposites), unless you sense them as one. Only by perceiving them as one can we sense the ratio between the high and low notes as one whole thing.

If things from different senses, like sweet and white, are even more different from each other than things from the same sense, like black and white, it is even less possible to sense them at the same time.

Therefore, if it's impossible to sense things from the same sense at the same time, it's even more impossible to sense things from different senses at the same time.

Some writers on musical harmony say that the sounds we hear together don't actually reach us at the same time but just seem to because the time between them is too small to notice. Is this true or not? Some might take this idea further and say that even when we think we see and hear things at the same time, it's just because the time difference is too small to notice. But this doesn't seem right. It's hard to believe that there could be a moment of time that is too small to notice because it's possible to sense every moment of time. This must be true because it's impossible for a person to be aware of themselves or anything else during continuous time without noticing each moment. If there were a moment of time that couldn't be noticed, then during that time, a person wouldn't be aware of themselves or what they were sensing, and that doesn't make sense.

If there were some amount of time or some object that was too small to sense, then you wouldn't actually be sensing anything during that time or sensing that object. You would only be sensing part of the object during part of the time. For example, if you imagine a line divided into two parts, and that line represents an object and a corresponding amount of time, if you are seeing the whole line, you are seeing it during the whole time. But if part of the time is cut off, you wouldn't be seeing anything during that time. So, you would only be seeing part of the object during part of the time, just like you only see part of the earth when you look at a specific area. But if you weren't seeing anything during one part of the time, then it doesn't make sense to say you saw the whole object during the whole time. This idea leads to the conclusion that you would never see the whole object during the whole time, which is absurd because it would mean you can never fully perceive anything.

Therefore, we have to conclude that all things can be sensed, but their exact size doesn't always appear right away when we sense them. For example, you can see the sun or a rod that is four cubits long from a distance, but you don't immediately know their exact size just by looking at them. Sometimes, something you see might seem like it has no size at all, but nothing you see is actually without size. We've already explained the reason for this. So, it's clear that no part of time is too small to be sensed.

Now, let's return to the original question: is it possible to sense multiple things at the same time? By "at the same time," I mean sensing several things in a single moment, where that moment is continuous and not divided.

First, is it possible to sense different things at the same time but with different parts of the soul? Or should we reject this idea? For example, if we assume the soul perceives one color with one part and another color with a different part, that would mean the soul has multiple parts that are the same in kind because the things it perceives are all colors.

If someone argues that just like we have two eyes, the soul could have something similar, the answer is that our two eyes work together as one organ, and that's why they perceive as one. If the soul is like this, then whatever part of the soul is formed by both would be the true perceiving subject. But if the two parts of the soul remain separate, the comparison with the eyes wouldn't work because the eyes function as one unit.

Furthermore, if the soul needed different parts to sense different things at the same time, each sense would be both one and many, like having different kinds of knowledge. But you can't have perception without the right kind of ability, and you can't have perception without an actual act of sensing.

If the soul doesn't sense multiple things at the same time with different parts, then it's even less likely that it senses things from different senses at the same time. As we've already said, it's more likely that the soul could sense multiple things from the same sense than from different senses.

If the soul uses one part to sense sweet and another part to sense white, then either these two parts form one whole or they don't. But there must be one whole because the general ability to sense is one. What single object does the soul sense when it perceives something that is both white and sweet? There isn't one because no single object is created from combining white and sweet. So, we have to conclude that the soul has one general ability to sense all things, but it uses different organs to sense different kinds of things.

Can we then say that the part of the soul that senses white and sweet is one when it acts as one and different when it acts as separate parts?

Or is the soul's way of perceiving things similar to how things themselves exist? The same thing can be both white and sweet and have many other qualities, while still being one thing. The qualities aren't actually separated in the object, but each quality exists in its own way. In the same way, the soul's ability to sense is one in number but different in kind. It is different in kind for some things and different in species for others. So, we can conclude that the soul can sense multiple things at the same time with one ability, but this ability changes depending on what it is sensing.

We can show that every object of sense has size and that nothing we sense is without size. For example, the distance from which you can't see something isn't a specific point, but the distance from which you can see it is. The same goes for smells, sounds, and all other things we sense without touching. There is a point in the distance where you can't see the object, and a point where you can see it. This point, where the object becomes visible, must be a specific spot. So, if any object were without size, it would have to be both visible and invisible at this point, but that's impossible.

This finishes our discussion of the characteristics of the organs of sense-perception and their objects. Next, we will consider the topics of memory and remembering.

• • •

On Life and Death

Aristotle's Inquiry into the Nature of Existence

A Modern Translation

Adapted for the Contemporary Reader

Aristotle

Translated by Tim Zengerink

Introduction

Ancient Greece was a civilization famous for its great contributions to philosophy, politics, art, and science. It thrived from the 8th century BCE until the Roman Empire started to decline. Greece's city-states, especially Athens, were the heart of culture and intellectual thought. This was the time when democracy began, impressive buildings like the Parthenon were built, and famous playwrights like Sophocles and Euripides produced their works. The Greeks' curiosity about the world around them laid the foundation for Western philosophy. Thinkers like Socrates, Plato, and later Aristotle, pushed the limits of what people understood about the world.

Greek society was deeply connected to theism, which focused on a large group of gods and goddesses who were believed to control every part of life. But this system did not prevent people from exploring new ideas. In fact, it coexisted with a growing interest in finding logical explanations for nature and human

life. Intellectuals would often debate and discuss these ideas in public places like the Agora. Aristotle grew up in this dynamic environment, learning from earlier philosophers, and later challenging and expanding their ideas.

Aristotle's Life

Aristotle was born in 384 BCE in a small town called Stagira, located in northern Greece. His father, Nicomachus, was a doctor for King Amyntas of Macedon, and this allowed Aristotle to be around the Macedonian royal court from a young age. When his parents passed away, Aristotle was sent to Athens at the age of 17 to pursue his education. Athens was the center of intellectual life in Greece, and Aristotle joined Plato's Academy, which was the most respected school of the time. The Academy was a place where students discussed everything from ethics to science. Although Aristotle learned a lot from Plato, he did not always agree with him, especially when it came to metaphysics, which deals with the nature of reality.

After spending almost 20 years at the Academy, Aristotle left Athens around 347 BCE after Plato's death. He traveled around different cities in Greece, continuing to study and learn. In 343 BCE, he was

invited to the court of King Philip II of Macedon, where he became the tutor of Philip's son, Alexander, who would later become known as Alexander the Great. Aristotle taught Alexander about philosophy, ethics, politics, and science. Aristotle's influence is visible in Alexander's leadership style, which showed respect for knowledge and strategic thinking.

After teaching Alexander, Aristotle returned to Athens in 335 BCE, where he opened his own school called the Lyceum. Unlike Plato's Academy, the Lyceum focused more on recording knowledge and observing nature. Aristotle and his students performed research, studied animals, and took notes on what they observed. The Lyceum became a major center of learning, and it rivaled Plato's Academy. This is also where Aristotle wrote many of his famous works.

Later in life, after the death of Alexander in 323 BCE, the political climate in Athens became difficult for Aristotle because of his connections to the Macedonian court. Accused of disrespecting the gods, Aristotle decided to leave Athens. He fled to Chalcis, where he passed away in 322 BCE. Even though he had to leave Athens, his legacy lived on through his many writings and the influence of his school, the Lyceum.

Aristotle's Impact on Western Thought

No figure looms larger over the development of Western philosophy and science than Aristotle. A student of Plato and tutor to Alexander the Great, he unified logic, ethics, politics, rhetoric, and metaphysics into a coherent system that shaped intellectual inquiry for centuries. Although his writings reflect the best knowledge of his era, they also reveal a distinctive way of understanding the world—one that balances observation with rigorous logical analysis. Over time, this method has profoundly influenced everything from political theory to modern scientific methodology.

Aristotle approached knowledge as an interconnected whole, seeing each field of study as a vital path toward truth. While many earlier thinkers focused on abstract concepts, he emphasized direct observation of the natural world. By systematically examining and classifying what he saw, Aristotle laid the groundwork for the empirical methods now central to modern science. Although our understanding of nature has evolved, his legacy endures in today's emphasis on evidence-based research.

Logic: The Foundation of Rational Inquiry

Often hailed as the "father of formal logic," Aristotle introduced a system of reasoning that shaped intellectual discourse for over two millennia. In works like the Organon, he analyzed how valid conclusions are drawn from premises and introduced syllogisms—deductive arguments that became standard tools in philosophy, theology, and science. Even contemporary logic, despite its modern mathematical and symbolic advancements, can trace many of its core principles back to Aristotle's pioneering analyses.

Metaphysics: Exploring the Nature of Reality

Aristotle's Metaphysics offered one of the earliest comprehensive explorations of existence at its most fundamental level. There, he described the nature of "being qua being" and introduced the concepts of potentiality and actuality to explain how things change and develop. These ideas deeply influenced medieval scholastics—both Christian and Islamic—who integrated Aristotelian reasoning into their theological frameworks. Today, discussions about consciousness, identity, and free will still reference these Aristotelian notions.

Ethics and the Pursuit of the Good Life

In the Nicomachean Ethics, Aristotle proposed that the ultimate aim of human life is eudaimonia, often translated as "happiness" or "flourishing." He argued that we achieve this through virtue, developed by cultivating good habits guided by reason. His famous Doctrine of the Mean asserts that moral virtue resides between two extremes—for instance, courage lies between recklessness and cowardice. This focus on character formation has profoundly shaped the tradition known as "virtue ethics," influencing modern debates on moral education, personal development, and what it means to live well.

Politics: The Role of the Individual in the City-State

Aristotle's practical approach to ethics naturally extended into political theory. In Politics, he explored various forms of government—monarchy, aristocracy, oligarchy, democracy—and weighed their merits and pitfalls. For Aristotle, a well-ordered polis (city-state) exists not merely for survival or trade but to enable its citizens to live virtuous, fulfilling lives. His conviction that ethics

and politics are intertwined remains influential, informing contemporary discussions on citizenship, governance, and justice.

Rhetoric: The Art of Persuasion

In his treatise Rhetoric, Aristotle examined how persuasion works, detailing how arguments must appeal to ethos (credibility), pathos (emotion), and logos (logic). This clear framework for effective communication continues to guide public speakers, legal advocates, and writers. From ancient courtroom orations to modern political campaigns, Aristotelian rhetoric underpins many of the strategies people use to sway audiences and shape public opinion.

Beyond these core subjects, Aristotle made significant contributions to biology, physics, psychology, and aesthetics. In the Poetics, for example, he investigated why humans respond so powerfully to tragic drama, pioneering the concept of catharsis—the emotional release that audiences feel through art. Throughout the medieval period, thinkers like Thomas Aquinas integrated Aristotle's theories into Christian theology, while Islamic philosophers such as Avicenna and Averroes preserved, interpreted, and expanded upon his works.

Across centuries of reinterpretation and debate, Aristotle remains a living voice in contemporary thought. His insistence on systematically gathering evidence and connecting it to logical principles laid the foundation for what we now recognize as the scientific method. His inquiries into human flourishing, civic responsibility, and the nature of argument continue to spark discussion and inspire new research. From personal ethics to societal organization, Aristotle's ideas help us frame enduring questions about how best to live, learn, and understand reality.

In sum, Aristotle stands as a foundational pillar of Western thought. He bridged abstract theorizing and practical inquiry, bequeathing a vision of knowledge that values both reason and experience. From ethics and politics to science and art, his ideas have been woven into countless intellectual traditions. Even today, as we grapple with questions of morality, governance, and truth, we walk in the footsteps of an ancient thinker whose breadth of insight and depth of analysis continue to guide our pursuit of wisdom.

Final Thoughts

By preserving Aristotle's legacy, we protect the intellectual depth and rigor that defined his way

of understanding the world. His systematic way of asking questions, his classification of knowledge, and his ethical theories are still relevant today, providing a model for critical thinking across many subjects. This preservation is important not just for philosophy students but for anyone interested in the foundations of human thought and the development of ideas that shape the world we live in.

One of the difficulties in studying Aristotle's work is that his ideas and language are complex. Translating these works into our modern language is a key step in making his profound insights easier for more people to understand. By putting his ideas into today's language, more readers can engage with his thoughts, even if they don't have a background in classical studies. Making Aristotle's work accessible means adapting them to modern ways of thinking without losing their original depth. This helps bridge the gap between ancient and modern readers, making sure Aristotle's work stays relevant.

Section 1

We now need to talk about youth, old age, life, and death. We will probably also need to explain the causes of breathing, since living and dying sometimes depend on it.

We have already explained the soul in detail elsewhere, and while it's clear that the soul itself isn't a physical thing, it must still exist in some part of the body that controls the other parts. Let's leave aside the other parts or abilities of the soul for now. When it comes to being an animal and being alive, we find that in all creatures that are both alive and animals, there is a single part that makes them both alive and animals. An animal cannot be an animal without being alive. However, something can be alive without being an animal, like plants, which live without feeling anything. It's through sensation that we tell the difference between animals and non-animals.

So, this part of the body that allows for life and being an animal must be the same in number but have different roles, because being alive and being an animal are not exactly the same thing. The organs of the different senses all connect to a single organ where all the senses meet when they work. This organ is located in the middle of the body, between what we call the front and the back (the front is where the senses come in, and the back is the opposite). Also, in all living things, the body is divided into upper and lower parts (even plants have upper and lower parts). This means the part of the body responsible for nutrition must be in the middle of these regions. We call the part where food comes in "the upper part" when we think of it by itself and not compared to the rest of the universe. The "lower part" is where waste is released.

Plants are the opposite of animals in this way. Humans, in particular, because of our upright posture, have our upper parts pointing upwards, like how the universe is structured. Other animals have their upper parts in a middle position. But in plants, because they are rooted in the ground and get their food from the soil, their upper part is always down. The roots of a plant are like the mouth of an animal, as this is where they take in food, whether it's from the earth or from another living thing.

All fully developed animals are divided into three parts: the part that takes in food, the part that releases waste, and the part that is in between. In larger animals, this middle part is called the chest, and in smaller animals, it's something similar. In some animals, this part is more clearly defined than in others. All animals that can move have extra body parts to help with this, such as legs or feet, which allow them to carry their whole body.

It's clear from both observation and reasoning that the source of the body's nourishment is in the middle of these three parts. Many animals can stay alive even when the head or the food container is cut off, as long as the middle part remains attached. This happens in many insects, like wasps and bees. Many other animals, besides insects, can also live after being cut in half as long as the part connected to nutrition remains.

While this middle part of the body is actually one organ, it has the potential to be multiple. These animals are similar to plants in this way. If you cut a plant into sections, each part can keep living, and you can grow multiple trees from one original plant. We will explain later why some plants can't survive when divided, while others can grow from cuttings. But in this way, plants and insects are alike.

The part of the body responsible for nourishment is actually one but has the potential to be many. This is also true for the part responsible for sensation, because the divided parts of these animals can still feel things. However, they can't maintain their structure like plants can because they don't have the organs needed to keep living. Some don't have the ability to grab food, while others can't digest it. They might also be missing other organs.

Animals that can be divided are like several animals growing together, but animals that are more complex are different because their bodies are united in the best possible way. This is why some organs, when divided, still show some sensation because they keep some life in them. For example, tortoises can keep moving even after their heart has been removed.

The same thing happens in both plants and animals. In plants, we see this when they grow from seeds, grafts, and cuttings. Growth from seeds always starts in the middle. All seeds have two halves, and the place where they join is where they attach to the plant, which is a middle part between the two sides. This middle part is where both the root and stem grow. So, the starting point is in the middle between the two. This is especially true for grafts and cuttings, which start growing from buds. The bud is the starting point of the branch and is located in the middle. When we graft a new plant or make a cutting, we either cut the bud or insert the new shoot into it because this is where new growth begins. This shows that growth starts in the middle, between the stem and the root.

In animals with blood, the heart is the first organ to develop. We know this from observing animals when possible. So, in animals without blood, the organ that is like the heart must also develop first. We've already said in our work on animal parts that veins come from the heart, and in animals with blood, the blood is the final nourishment that forms the body parts. This shows that the mouth plays one role in nutrition, and the stomach plays another, but the heart is in control and completes the process. So, in animals with blood, the source of both sensation and nutrition must be in the heart, because the other organs involved in nutrition only help the heart in its work. The main organ is responsible for completing the process, just like how a doctor's goal is to bring about health, not just to focus on smaller tasks.

In all animals with blood, the main organ for sensation is the heart, because this is where the common center for all the senses is located. This is clear for taste and touch because they can be directly connected to the heart. So, the other senses must also lead to the heart, since the heart is where changes start in the other sense organs, while the senses in the head, like taste and touch, are not connected to the heart. Also, if life is always located in the heart, then the source of sensation must also be there. An animal is called "alive" because it can sense things, and we call something an animal because it can feel. In other works, we've explained why some of the senses are connected to the heart and others are in the head. (This is why some people think that sensation comes from the brain.)

If we look at the facts, it's clear that the source of the sensitive soul, along with the part responsible for growth and nutrition, is located in the heart, which is in the middle of the body. This also makes sense from reasoning. In every case, Nature always chooses the best outcome when possible. If both the sensitive and the nutritive principles are located in the middle of the body, the parts responsible for processing food and the parts that receive food will work best. This is because the soul will be close to both, and the central position it holds is the place of control.

The thing that uses a tool and the tool itself must be different. If possible, they should also be separate in space, just like a flute and the hand that plays it. So, if an animal is defined by its ability to sense, this ability must be located in the heart in animals with blood, and in a similar part in animals without blood. In all animals, the body and its parts have some natural warmth, which is why they are warm when alive and cold when dead. This warmth must come from the heart in animals with blood, and from a similar organ in animals without blood. While all parts of the body use their natural heat to process food, the main organ plays the biggest role in this process. This is why life continues even when other parts of the body become cold. But when the warmth in this main organ is gone, death always follows because the heat in all the other parts depends on this organ. The soul is like a fire in this part of the body, which is the heart in animals with blood, and a similar organ in animals without blood. So, life depends on maintaining this heat, and death happens when this heat is destroyed.

It's important to note that fire can stop burning in two ways: either it goes out on its own or something else puts it out. When it stops by itself, we call it exhaustion, and when something else puts it out, we call it extinction. Fire can go out either way from the same cause. When there isn't enough fuel and the heat can't keep burning, the fire dies out. This happens because something blocks digestion and stops the fire from being fed. In other cases, the fire burns out from exhaustion—when heat builds up too much because there's no way to cool down or breathe. In this situation, the heat quickly uses up all its fuel before more can come in. This is why a small fire can be put out by a bigger one, and a candle flame gets swallowed up when placed in a large fire, just like any other burnable material. The bigger fire uses up the fuel before more can be added. Fire is always being created and moving forward, like a river, but it happens so fast we don't notice.

So, if the body's heat needs to be kept steady (which it does to stay alive), there has to be a way to cool down the source of heat. Think of what happens when you cover hot coals in a container. If they stay covered for too long, they burn out. But if you keep lifting the lid and putting it back down quickly, the coals will stay hot for a long time. Piling ashes on a fire also keeps it going, because ashes are porous and allow air to pass through, while also keeping the heat from escaping into the surrounding air. In our work *The Problems*, we've explained why covering a fire makes it go out, while piling ashes on it keeps it burning for a long time.

Everything that is alive has a soul, and as we've said, the soul can't exist without heat in the body. In plants, the natural heat is kept alive by the food they take in and the air around them. Food cools the body when it first enters, just like in humans. When a plant doesn't get food, it produces heat and becomes thirsty. Air, if it doesn't move, becomes hot, but when food enters, it causes movement, which continues until digestion is done, and this cools the body. If the air around the plant is too cold because of the season, the plant withers. Or if, in the heat of summer, the moisture from the ground can't cool the plant, the heat in the plant burns out. When this happens, we say the plants are scorched or burned by the sun. That's why people sometimes put stones or pots of water under the roots of plants to keep them cool.

Some animals live in water, while others live in the air. These environments provide the cooling they need—water for the ones in water, and air for those in the air. We will need to explain more about how exactly this cooling happens.

A few of the early philosophers talked about breathing. But they either didn't explain why animals breathe, or they gave incorrect explanations, showing they didn't know the facts very well. They also wrongly said that all animals breathe, which isn't true. So, we need to address these points first so we don't seem like we're criticizing those who are no longer alive without reason.

First, it's clear that all animals with lungs breathe. But in some animals, the lungs don't have much blood and are more like sponges, so they don't need to breathe as much. These animals can stay underwater for a long time, relative to their strength. All egg-laying animals, like frogs, have lungs like sponges. Tortoises can also stay underwater for a long time because their lungs don't hold much blood and don't produce much heat. Once their lungs fill with air, the movement of the lungs cools the animal and allows it to stay underwater for a while. However, if an animal holds its breath for too long, it will suffocate, because none of these animals can take in water the way fish do. On the other hand, animals with lungs full of blood need to breathe more because they have more heat. Animals without lungs don't breathe at all.

Democritus and others who wrote about breathing didn't say much about animals without lungs, but they seemed to think that all animals breathe. Anaxagoras and Diogenes both said that all animals breathe, and they tried to explain how fish and oysters breathe. Anaxagoras said that when fish push water through their gills, air forms in their mouths, because there can't be a vacuum. He thought they breathe by taking in this air. Diogenes said that when fish push water out through their gills, they suck air from the water into their mouths because a vacuum is formed in the mouth. He believed there was air in the water.

But these ideas don't work. They only describe part of what's going on and leave out the rest. Breathing involves both inhaling and exhaling air, but these explanations don't say anything about how these animals breathe out. They can't explain it because these animals would have to breathe out through the same passage they breathe in. This would mean that they would have to take water into their mouths while breathing out at the same time. But the air and water would meet and block each other. When the animal pushes water out, it would also have to push out its breath through the mouth or gills. As a result, it would be breathing in and out at the same time, which is impossible. So, if breathing means both inhaling and exhaling air, and these animals can't breathe out, then they can't breathe at all.

Also, the idea that fish breathe by pulling air from the water with their mouths is impossible because they don't have lungs or windpipes. Instead, their stomachs are close to their mouths, so they would have to suck air into their stomachs. If that were true, other animals would do the same, but they don't. Fish also don't do this when they're out of the water, which is obvious. In animals that breathe, you can see movement in the part of the body that pulls in air, but fish don't show any movement in their stomachs, only in their gills. Their gills move both when they are in the water and when they are on land gasping for air. Also, when animals that breathe are drowned, they release air bubbles as the air is forced out, like when a tortoise or frog is held underwater. But this never happens with fish, no matter how we try, because they don't take in air from outside.

If fish really breathed by pulling in air from the water, people should be able to do the same when they are underwater. If fish pull in air through their mouths, why couldn't humans or other animals do that too? But since humans can't do it, neither can fish. Also, why do fish die in the air and gasp as if they are suffocating? It's not because they lack food, and Diogenes' explanation is ridiculous. He says fish die because they take in too much air when out of the water, but in water, they take in just the right amount. But if that were true, land animals should also be able to suffocate from breathing too much air. But that doesn't happen. If all animals breathe, then insects must breathe too. Some insects, like centipedes, seem to live even after being cut into several pieces. How can they breathe when divided, and what organs do they use?

The reason these philosophers gave bad explanations is that they didn't understand the internal organs and didn't believe that everything in nature has a purpose. If they had asked what the purpose of breathing is and thought about the organs involved, like the lungs and gills, they would have figured it out sooner.

Democritus, however, did say that breathing has a purpose. He said it keeps the soul from being pushed out of the body. But he didn't say that nature designed breathing for this purpose. Like the other early philosophers, he didn't reach this level of understanding. He said the soul and heat are the same thing, made up of small, round particles. When the air around us presses on the body and tries to push the soul out, breathing helps prevent this. Democritus thought the air contains many particles of soul and mind, and when we breathe in, these particles enter the body and push back against the pressure, keeping the soul in place.

This is why, he said, life and death are connected to breathing in and out. Death happens when the pressure from the air around us becomes too strong, and the animal can no longer breathe in. At that point, the air can't get in to balance the pressure, and the soul is pushed out of the body. Death, according to him, is the result of the soul being forced out by the pressure of the air around us. Death happens naturally with old age, or unnaturally through violence.

But Democritus didn't explain why death happens or why everything must eventually die. He should have explained whether the cause of death is internal or external, especially since death happens at certain times in life and not others. He also didn't explain where breathing begins or whether its cause is internal or external. It's not true that the air outside controls breathing. The cause of breathing must come from within the body, not from pressure outside. It's also strange to think that the air around us would both squeeze the body and, by entering, expand it at the same time. This is Democritus' theory and how he explains it.

But if our earlier explanation is correct, and not all animals breathe, then Democritus' explanation of death applies only to animals that breathe, not to all animals. And even for animals that breathe, his explanation isn't correct, as we can see from experience. In hot weather, when we get warmer and need to breathe more, we breathe faster. But when the air around us is cold, it shrinks and tightens the body, which slows down breathing. At this time, the outside air should enter the body and cancel out the pressure, but the opposite happens. When we can't breathe out and the heat inside builds up too much, we need to breathe, which means we need to take in air. In hot weather, people breathe faster to cool down, even though Democritus' theory would suggest that they should be adding more heat to their bodies.

The idea from *Timaeus* about breathing, where air is pushed around in the body, doesn't explain how heat is kept in animals other than those that live on land. It also doesn't say if their heat comes from the same or a different source. If breathing only happens in land animals, we should be told why. If other animals also breathe but in a different way, then this form of breathing needs to be explained, assuming all animals breathe.

Also, the explanation seems made up. It says that when hot air leaves the mouth, it pushes the air around it, which then enters the body again through the pores of the skin, filling the place where the warm air came out. This happens because a vacuum (empty space) can't exist. Then, when the air heats up, it leaves the body again through the same route and pushes the warm air back inside through the mouth. They say this process happens continuously when we breathe in and out.

But with this explanation, it would mean we breathe out before we breathe in, which isn't true. The opposite is what really happens, as we can observe. Even though breathing in and out alternates, the last thing we do before death is exhale, so the first act must have been to inhale.

Also, those who explain breathing like this don't say why animals have this function. They make it sound like breathing just happens as part of being alive, but it clearly has control over life and death. When an animal can't breathe, it dies. It's also strange to suggest that the hot air leaving the body is easy to notice, but we can't detect the air entering the lungs and heating up again. It's even more ridiculous to think that breathing involves taking in heat when the opposite is true: we breathe out hot air and take in cool air. When it's hot, we pant because the air coming in isn't cooling us enough, so we have to breathe more frequently.

But we shouldn't think that breathing is for feeding the body like food. Breathing isn't about adding fuel to the body's internal fire, as some have said, with the air acting like food for the flame and then being breathed out. I'll repeat the argument I used earlier against this idea. If that were true, we would see the same thing happening in other animals since they all have body heat. Also, how could breathing create heat? We see that heat comes from food, not air. This theory would also mean that the same passage in the body would be used for taking in food and pushing out waste, but we don't see that happening in other cases.

Empedocles also explained breathing, but he didn't make clear what its purpose is or whether it's universal in all animals. He talked about breathing through the nostrils as if it were the main kind of breathing. But the air that enters through the nostrils also passes through the windpipe and out of the chest, and without the windpipe, the nostrils can't function. Also, if an animal can't breathe through its nose, it's fine. But if it can't breathe through its windpipe, it dies. Nature uses nose breathing for smelling in some animals. The reason why only some animals have it is that, while most animals can smell, they don't all have the same organs for it.

Empedocles also described how breathing works by saying that certain blood vessels hold blood but are not filled with it. These vessels have openings that connect to the air outside the body. The openings are small enough to keep the solid parts of the blood in but large enough for air to pass through. He said that when the blood moves down, air comes in, and this causes inhaling. When the blood moves up, air is pushed out, causing exhaling. He compared this to a water clock, a device used to measure time with water.

Here's how he explained it:

"All things breathe in and out. Their bodies have small tubes that reach the outer edges. These tubes have many channels leading through the nostrils. When the blood moves away, air rushes in. But when the blood moves up, air flows out. This is like a water clock. When a girl puts her hand over the tube and dips it in water, no water enters because the air is trapped. But when she lets the air escape, water rushes in. Just like the water clock, the blood moves, creating space for the air to flow in or out."

That's how he explained breathing. But as we've said, all animals that breathe do so through their windpipe, whether they breathe through their mouth or nose. If he's talking about this kind of breathing, we need to ask how it matches his explanation. The facts seem to go against it. The chest rises like a bellows when we inhale. It makes sense that heat would lift it up and that the blood would gather in the warm area. But the chest sinks back down when we exhale, just like a bellows. The difference is that in breathing, the air comes in and goes out through the same passage, while in a bellows, the air enters and exits through different places.

If Empedocles is only talking about breathing through the nose, he's mistaken. Nose breathing doesn't just involve the nostrils; it also passes through the area near the uvula, at the roof of the mouth. Some of the air goes through the nostrils, and some goes through the mouth, both when we breathe in and when we breathe out.

These are the problems with how other philosophers have explained breathing.

• • •

On Breathing

Understanding the Connection Between Breath and Life

A Modern Translation

Adapted for the Contemporary Reader

Aristotle

Translated by Tim Zengerink

Introduction

Ancient Greece was a civilization famous for its great contributions to philosophy, politics, art, and science. It thrived from the 8th century BCE until the Roman Empire started to decline. Greece's city-states, especially Athens, were the heart of culture and intellectual thought. This was the time when democracy began, impressive buildings like the Parthenon were built, and famous playwrights like Sophocles and Euripides produced their works. The Greeks' curiosity about the world around them laid the foundation for Western philosophy. Thinkers like Socrates, Plato, and later Aristotle, pushed the limits of what people understood about the world.

Greek society was deeply connected to theism, which focused on a large group of gods and goddesses who were believed to control every part of life. But this system did not prevent people from exploring new ideas. In fact, it coexisted with a growing interest in finding logical explanations for nature and human

life. Intellectuals would often debate and discuss these ideas in public places like the Agora. Aristotle grew up in this dynamic environment, learning from earlier philosophers, and later challenging and expanding their ideas.

Aristotle's Life

Aristotle was born in 384 BCE in a small town called Stagira, located in northern Greece. His father, Nicomachus, was a doctor for King Amyntas of Macedon, and this allowed Aristotle to be around the Macedonian royal court from a young age. When his parents passed away, Aristotle was sent to Athens at the age of 17 to pursue his education. Athens was the center of intellectual life in Greece, and Aristotle joined Plato's Academy, which was the most respected school of the time. The Academy was a place where students discussed everything from ethics to science. Although Aristotle learned a lot from Plato, he did not always agree with him, especially when it came to metaphysics, which deals with the nature of reality.

After spending almost 20 years at the Academy, Aristotle left Athens around 347 BCE after Plato's death. He traveled around different cities in Greece, continuing to study and learn. In 343 BCE, he was

invited to the court of King Philip II of Macedon, where he became the tutor of Philip's son, Alexander, who would later become known as Alexander the Great. Aristotle taught Alexander about philosophy, ethics, politics, and science. Aristotle's influence is visible in Alexander's leadership style, which showed respect for knowledge and strategic thinking.

After teaching Alexander, Aristotle returned to Athens in 335 BCE, where he opened his own school called the Lyceum. Unlike Plato's Academy, the Lyceum focused more on recording knowledge and observing nature. Aristotle and his students performed research, studied animals, and took notes on what they observed. The Lyceum became a major center of learning, and it rivaled Plato's Academy. This is also where Aristotle wrote many of his famous works.

Later in life, after the death of Alexander in 323 BCE, the political climate in Athens became difficult for Aristotle because of his connections to the Macedonian court. Accused of disrespecting the gods, Aristotle decided to leave Athens. He fled to Chalcis, where he passed away in 322 BCE. Even though he had to leave Athens, his legacy lived on through his many writings and the influence of his school, the Lyceum.

Aristotle's Impact on Western Thought

No figure looms larger over the development of Western philosophy and science than Aristotle. A student of Plato and tutor to Alexander the Great, he unified logic, ethics, politics, rhetoric, and metaphysics into a coherent system that shaped intellectual inquiry for centuries. Although his writings reflect the best knowledge of his era, they also reveal a distinctive way of understanding the world—one that balances observation with rigorous logical analysis. Over time, this method has profoundly influenced everything from political theory to modern scientific methodology.

Aristotle approached knowledge as an interconnected whole, seeing each field of study as a vital path toward truth. While many earlier thinkers focused on abstract concepts, he emphasized direct observation of the natural world. By systematically examining and classifying what he saw, Aristotle laid the groundwork for the empirical methods now central to modern science. Although our understanding of nature has evolved, his legacy endures in today's emphasis on evidence-based research.

Logic: The Foundation of Rational Inquiry

Often hailed as the "father of formal logic," Aristotle introduced a system of reasoning that shaped intellectual discourse for over two millennia. In works like the Organon, he analyzed how valid conclusions are drawn from premises and introduced syllogisms—deductive arguments that became standard tools in philosophy, theology, and science. Even contemporary logic, despite its modern mathematical and symbolic advancements, can trace many of its core principles back to Aristotle's pioneering analyses.

Metaphysics: Exploring the Nature of Reality

Aristotle's Metaphysics offered one of the earliest comprehensive explorations of existence at its most fundamental level. There, he described the nature of "being qua being" and introduced the concepts of potentiality and actuality to explain how things change and develop. These ideas deeply influenced medieval scholastics—both Christian and Islamic—who integrated Aristotelian reasoning into their theological frameworks. Today, discussions about consciousness, identity, and free will still reference these Aristotelian notions.

Ethics and the Pursuit of the Good Life

In the Nicomachean Ethics, Aristotle proposed that the ultimate aim of human life is eudaimonia, often translated as "happiness" or "flourishing." He argued that we achieve this through virtue, developed by cultivating good habits guided by reason. His famous Doctrine of the Mean asserts that moral virtue resides between two extremes—for instance, courage lies between recklessness and cowardice. This focus on character formation has profoundly shaped the tradition known as "virtue ethics," influencing modern debates on moral education, personal development, and what it means to live well.

Politics: The Role of the Individual in the City-State

Aristotle's practical approach to ethics naturally extended into political theory. In Politics, he explored various forms of government—monarchy, aristocracy, oligarchy, democracy—and weighed their merits and pitfalls. For Aristotle, a well-ordered polis (city-state) exists not merely for survival or trade but to enable its citizens to live virtuous, fulfilling lives. His conviction that ethics

and politics are intertwined remains influential, informing contemporary discussions on citizenship, governance, and justice.

Rhetoric: The Art of Persuasion

In his treatise Rhetoric, Aristotle examined how persuasion works, detailing how arguments must appeal to ethos (credibility), pathos (emotion), and logos (logic). This clear framework for effective communication continues to guide public speakers, legal advocates, and writers. From ancient courtroom orations to modern political campaigns, Aristotelian rhetoric underpins many of the strategies people use to sway audiences and shape public opinion.

Beyond these core subjects, Aristotle made significant contributions to biology, physics, psychology, and aesthetics. In the Poetics, for example, he investigated why humans respond so powerfully to tragic drama, pioneering the concept of catharsis—the emotional release that audiences feel through art. Throughout the medieval period, thinkers like Thomas Aquinas integrated Aristotle's theories into Christian theology, while Islamic philosophers such as Avicenna and Averroes preserved, interpreted, and expanded upon his works.

Across centuries of reinterpretation and debate, Aristotle remains a living voice in contemporary thought. His insistence on systematically gathering evidence and connecting it to logical principles laid the foundation for what we now recognize as the scientific method. His inquiries into human flourishing, civic responsibility, and the nature of argument continue to spark discussion and inspire new research. From personal ethics to societal organization, Aristotle's ideas help us frame enduring questions about how best to live, learn, and understand reality.

In sum, Aristotle stands as a foundational pillar of Western thought. He bridged abstract theorizing and practical inquiry, bequeathing a vision of knowledge that values both reason and experience. From ethics and politics to science and art, his ideas have been woven into countless intellectual traditions. Even today, as we grapple with questions of morality, governance, and truth, we walk in the footsteps of an ancient thinker whose breadth of insight and depth of analysis continue to guide our pursuit of wisdom.

Final Thoughts

By preserving Aristotle's legacy, we protect the intellectual depth and rigor that defined his way

of understanding the world. His systematic way of asking questions, his classification of knowledge, and his ethical theories are still relevant today, providing a model for critical thinking across many subjects. This preservation is important not just for philosophy students but for anyone interested in the foundations of human thought and the development of ideas that shape the world we live in.

One of the difficulties in studying Aristotle's work is that his ideas and language are complex. Translating these works into our modern language is a key step in making his profound insights easier for more people to understand. By putting his ideas into today's language, more readers can engage with his thoughts, even if they don't have a background in classical studies. Making Aristotle's work accessible means adapting them to modern ways of thinking without losing their original depth. This helps bridge the gap between ancient and modern readers, making sure Aristotle's work stays relevant.

Section 1

We have already mentioned that life and the presence of a soul involve a certain warmth. Even the process of digesting food, which provides nutrition for animals, doesn't happen without the soul and warmth, because in all cases, digestion is due to heat. That's why the main part of the soul responsible for nutrition must be located in the part of the body where this principle is active. This part is between where food enters and where waste is expelled. In animals without blood, this part doesn't have a name, but in animals with blood, it's called the heart. The blood provides the nourishment from which the animal's organs are made. So, the blood vessels must have the same starting point since they exist to support the blood by serving as its containers. In animals with blood, the heart is where the veins start; they don't pass through it, but instead, they spread out from it, as we can see when we study dissections.

Other abilities of the soul can't exist without the power of nutrition (as explained in the treatise *On the Soul*), and this power depends on natural heat, which Nature has activated by bringing it to life. But fire, as we have already said, can be destroyed in two ways—by going out or burning out. It can be put out by its opposite forces. So, fire can be extinguished by surrounding cold, whether it's in large amounts or spread out (though it happens faster when spread out). This kind of destruction happens by force both in living and non-living things, for cutting an animal apart or freezing it with extreme cold causes death. However, burning out happens when there is too much heat; if the heat is too intense and nothing adds new fuel, the fire will go out because it burns out, not because of cold. So, if it's going to keep going, it needs to be cooled down because cold prevents this kind of burnout.

Some animals live in water, while others live on land. For very small, bloodless animals, the cooling effect of the surrounding water or air is enough to prevent them from burning out due to heat. Since they don't have much heat, they don't need much cold to keep them balanced. This also explains why these animals don't live long, because being small means they have less ability to resist extremes. But some insects live longer, even though they are bloodless like the others, and they have a deep indentation below their middle section to allow cooling through a thinner membrane. These insects are warmer and need more cooling, like bees (some of which live for seven years) and all insects that make a humming noise, such as wasps, beetles, and crickets. They make a sound that's like panting by using air, as the air inside them causes a rising and falling movement that creates friction against the membrane. The way they move this area is similar to how the lungs move in animals that breathe, or how gills move in fish. What happens is like when an animal that breathes air is suffocated by blocking its mouth, causing the lungs to make a similar rising and falling movement. In these animals, this internal movement isn't enough for cooling, but in insects, it is. By creating friction against the membrane, they make the humming sound, as we said, similar to how children make sounds by blowing through a reed covered by a thin membrane. This is also how crickets make their songs; they have more heat and a deeper indentation at the waist, while those that don't make noise have no such indentation.

Animals that have blood and lungs, but whose lungs have little blood and are spongy, can sometimes live for a long time without breathing, because the lung, with its small amount of blood or liquid, can rise very high, and its own movement can keep cooling the body for a long time. But eventually, this is not enough, and the animal dies from suffocation if it doesn't breathe, as we've already mentioned. Exhaustion due to a lack of cooling is called suffocation, and anything that dies this way is said to be suffocated.

We've already said that insects don't breathe like other animals, and we can observe this in small creatures like flies and bees, which can move around in a liquid for a long time as long as it's not too hot or cold. However, animals with little strength tend to breathe more often. These animals die from what we call suffocation when their stomach fills up and the heat in their middle part is lost. This is also why they can revive after being in ashes for some time.

Among water animals, those without blood can live longer in air than those with blood, like fish. Since they have a small amount of heat, the air can cool them for a long time, as we see in animals like crabs and octopuses. However, the air is not enough to keep them alive because they don't have enough heat. Many fish can also live in the soil, though they stay still, and they can be found by digging. All animals that don't have lungs or have bloodless lungs need less cooling.

Regarding bloodless animals, we've explained that some rely on the surrounding air and others on fluids to maintain life. But for animals with blood and a heart, all those with lungs take in air and cool themselves by breathing in and out. All animals that give birth to live young and do so inside their bodies (unlike the Selachia, which give birth outside) have lungs, as do oviparous animals, such as birds and scaly animals like tortoises, lizards, and snakes. In the first group, the lungs are filled with blood, but in most of the latter, the lungs are spongy. So, they breathe less often, as we've said before. This function is also found in animals that live in water, like water snakes, frogs, crocodiles, and turtles, whether they live in the sea or on land, as well as in seals.

All these animals give birth on land and sleep on land, or when they sleep in water, they keep their heads above the surface to breathe. But animals with gills cool themselves by taking in water; this includes Selachia and other animals without legs. Fish have no legs, and their fins are named for their resemblance to wings. However, one animal with legs, the tadpole, has gills.

No animal has both lungs and gills, and the reason is that lungs are made for cooling through air (their name, "pneumon," seems to come from their function as a container for breath), while gills are for cooling through water. Since one tool is enough for one purpose, Nature doesn't make unnecessary organs. So, some animals have gills, others have lungs, but none have both.

Every animal needs food to live and cooling to prevent death. Nature uses the same organ for both tasks. For example, in some animals, the tongue is used both to taste food and for speaking. In animals with lungs, the mouth is used to break down food and to let air in and out. In animals without lungs or that don't breathe, the mouth is just used to break down food, while in animals that need cooling, gills are made for this purpose.

We'll explain later how these organs produce cooling. But to make sure food doesn't interfere with breathing, both respiring animals and those that take in water have a similar system. When they breathe, they don't take in food, because food, whether liquid or dry, could get into the windpipe and cause suffocation by blocking the lungs. The windpipe is located in front of the esophagus, through which food goes into the stomach. In blooded quadrupeds, there is a lid called the epiglottis over the windpipe. In birds and egg-laying quadrupeds, this covering is missing, but they close their windpipes by contracting them. When swallowing food, birds contract the windpipe while mammals close the epiglottis. Once the food has passed, the epiglottis is raised, or the windpipe expands, allowing air to enter and cool the body. In animals with gills, water is expelled first, then food enters the mouth. They don't have a windpipe, so they aren't harmed by liquids entering their windpipe, only by liquids entering the stomach. This is why these animals quickly expel water and grab their food. Their teeth are sharp and often arranged like a saw because they can't chew their food.

Among water animals, cetaceans, like dolphins and whales, may seem puzzling, but they can be explained. Examples of these animals include dolphins, whales, and others with blowholes. They don't have legs but do have lungs, even though they live in water. They have lungs for cooling, as we mentioned, but they don't take in water to cool themselves. Instead, they cool down by breathing because they have lungs. That's why they sleep with their heads out of the water, and dolphins even snore. If they get caught in nets, they die quickly from suffocation because they can't breathe. So, they can be seen coming to the surface to breathe. Since they need to eat in the water, they take in water and expel it through their blowholes, just as fish expel water through their gills. The blowhole is placed in front of the brain, where it releases the water without touching any of the blood-filled organs.

Mollusks and crustaceans, like crabs, also take in water for the same reason. These animals don't need cooling because they don't have much heat and are bloodless. The surrounding water cools them enough. But when they eat, they take in water, and they have to expel it to avoid swallowing it along with the food. Crustaceans, like crabs and lobsters, expel water through the folds beside their hairy parts, while cuttlefish and octopuses use the hollow above their heads. There's a more detailed explanation of these animals in *The History of Animals*.

This explains why animals take in water for cooling and how those that live in water must eat in it as well.

We must now explain how cooling happens in animals that breathe and those with gills. We've already said that all animals with lungs breathe. The reason some creatures have lungs, and those that do need to breathe, is that higher animals have more heat. Since they have a higher soul and nature than plants, they need this. Animals with more blood and warmth in their lungs tend to be larger, and the animal with the purest and most abundant blood in the lungs is the most upright—this is man. The reason man alone stands with his upper part directed toward the upper part of the universe is that he has such lungs.

So, the lungs must be considered an essential part of the animal's nature, both in humans and in other animals.

This is the purpose of cooling. As for the cause behind this, we must believe that nature made animals this way, just as it made many other animals with different compositions. Some animals have more earth in their makeup, like plants, while others, like aquatic animals, have more water. Winged and land animals have more air and fire, respectively. Each thing exists in the region that suits the element most abundant in its composition.

Empedocles was wrong when he said that animals with the most warmth and fire live in water to balance the heat in their bodies. He thought that since they lack cold and fluid, living in water keeps them alive, as water has less heat than air. But it makes no sense that water animals would all originate on land and then move to the water, especially since most of them have no legs. Yet, he said that they were first created on land and then moved to the water. But it's clear that water animals aren't warmer than land animals, as some have no blood at all, and others have very little.

We've already discussed what kinds of animals should be considered warm and what kinds cold. While

Empedocles' idea has some logic, his explanation is wrong. A condition that is too extreme is balanced by its opposite, but the best way for an animal's body to stay healthy is to be in an environment similar to its own nature. There's a difference between what an animal is made of and the condition of that material. For example, if nature made something out of wax or ice, it wouldn't be kept safe in a hot place because heat would quickly destroy it, as heat melts what cold freezes. Likewise, something made of salt or nitre wouldn't be placed in water because water would dissolve it, as its structure depends on being dry and warm.

So, if all bodies are made of wet and dry materials, it makes sense that things made mostly of wet and cold elements would live in liquid environments. And if they are cold, they would exist in cold places, while things made mostly of dry elements would be found on land. Trees, for instance, don't grow in water but on dry land. But according to Empedocles' theory, they should live in water because they are so dry, just like things that are very fiery. They would move to water, not because of the cold, but because of its fluid nature.

In reality, the natural state of materials is suited to the regions they exist in. Liquids belong in liquid environments, dry things on land, and warm things in the air. However, in terms of a body's condition, a cold environment helps balance out too much heat, while a warm one helps balance too much cold. The region around the animal adjusts the excess condition in its body. The regions where things live and the changing seasons also help fix such imbalances. But while a body's condition can be the opposite of its surroundings, the material that makes up the body cannot be. This explains why some animals are aquatic and others are terrestrial, and why some have lungs while others do not. It's not because of the amount of heat in their bodies, as Empedocles claimed.

The reason animals with lungs, especially those with lungs full of blood, breathe air is because the lungs are spongy and full of tubes. The lungs also have more blood than any other organ. All animals with blood-filled lungs need to cool down quickly because they don't have much room for changes in their body heat. The air needs to get through the entire lung because of the large amount of blood and heat it holds. Air can easily do this because it's light and can spread everywhere quickly, allowing it to cool down the body. Water, on the other hand, can't do this as easily.

This explains why animals with blood-filled lungs breathe more often—the more heat they have, the more cooling they need. Also, air can easily reach the source of heat in the heart.

To understand how the heart connects to the lungs through passages, we should look at dissections and the information in the *History of Animals*. The main reason animals need cooling is that the soul and fire come together in the heart. Breathing is how animals with lungs and a heart cool themselves. But for animals like fish, which live in water and don't have lungs, cooling happens through the gills using water. If you want to see how the heart connects to the gills, you need to look at dissections, and for more details, refer to *Natural History*. For now, we can sum it up like this.

It might seem like the heart is in a different position in land animals and fish, but the position is actually the same. The tip of the heart points in the direction the animal tilts its head. In fish, the tip of the heart points toward the mouth, since they don't tilt their heads the same way land animals do. From the tip of the heart, a large, strong tube runs to the center where all the gills meet. This is the biggest tube, but there are others on either side of the heart that go to each gill. Water constantly flows through the gills, cooling the heart.

In the same way fish move their gills, animals that breathe raise and lower their chest as they inhale and exhale. If there isn't enough fresh air, or if the air isn't replaced, they suffocate because the air, after touching the blood, heats up quickly. The heat from the blood cancels out the cooling effect, and when animals can't move their lungs (or fish can't move their gills) due to sickness or old age, they die.

Being born and dying are common to all animals, but there are different ways these things happen. There are different types of death, though they all have something in common. There is violent death, caused by something outside the body, and natural death, caused by something inside the body, built into the way the body is made. It's not something that comes from outside. For plants, this is called withering; for animals, it's called aging. Death and decay happen to everything that is fully developed, though it can also happen to things that aren't fully developed, like eggs or seeds before they sprout roots.

Death always happens due to a loss of heat, and in fully developed creatures, this happens when heat runs out in the organ that is the source of the creature's essential life. As we've said, this organ is located between the upper and lower parts of the body. In plants, it's between the root and the stem, and in animals with blood, it's the heart. In bloodless animals, it's the equivalent part of their body. Some animals have many potential sources of life, though they actually have only one. This explains why some insects can keep living even when they are cut in half, and why even some animals with blood can live for a long time after their heart is removed. For example, tortoises can still move their legs as long as they have their shell, which is due to their naturally weaker constitution, as we see in insects too.

Life ends when the heat that sustains it is no longer cooled properly. As I've said before, the heat burns itself up. So, when the lungs in one type of animal, or the gills in another, dry out over time, they become hard and earthy, unable to move. They can't expand or contract anymore. Eventually, the fire goes out due to exhaustion.

This is why even a small disturbance can cause death in old age. There isn't much heat left because most of it has been used up over the long life. Any extra strain on the body can quickly extinguish what's left. It's like the heart contains a small, weak flame that can easily be put out by the slightest movement. This is why death in old age is painless—there's no need for a violent event to cause it, and the soul departs quietly without feeling anything. Diseases that harden the lungs, such as tumors or excess heat from fevers, speed up breathing because the lungs can't move much either up or down. When the lungs can't move at all, breathing stops, and death follows.

Being born is when an animal first shares in the life-giving soul through warmth, and life is the process of keeping this connection. Youth is the time when the organ for cooling grows, old age is when it starts to decay, and the time in between is the prime of life.

A violent death happens when the vital heat is put out or burns out (both can cause death), while natural death happens when the heat runs out over time and life ends. For plants, this is called withering; for animals, it's called dying. In old age, death is caused by the body's inability to keep cooling itself due to the passage of time. This is our explanation of birth, life, and death, and why they happen in animals.

It is clear why animals that breathe air suffocate in water, and why fish suffocate in air. For fish, water provides the cooling they need, while for animals that breathe air, the air does the same. When either is taken away by a change in their environment, the function is lost.

We must also explain why gills and lungs move the way they do, and how this movement allows air or water to come in and go out. Here's how these organs are structured.

There are three things related to the heart that might seem similar but are actually different: palpitation, pulsation, and respiration.

Palpitation happens when the hot substance in the heart rushes together due to the cooling effect of waste products. This happens in conditions like spasms and other illnesses. It also occurs when you're scared, because when you're afraid, the upper parts of your body become cold, and the hot substance retreats to the heart. This causes the heart to palpitate because the heat is squeezed into such a small space that sometimes life is extinguished, and animals can die from fear and the disturbance it causes.

The constant beating of the heart is similar to the throbbing of an abscess. However, an abscess is painful because the blood changes in an unnatural way, and the throbbing continues until the matter inside is discharged. This process is similar to boiling, where heat turns liquid into vapor and expands it. But in an abscess, if nothing evaporates, the liquid thickens, and the process ends in the formation of pus. In boiling, it ends with the liquid escaping from the container.

In the heart, the beating is caused by heat expanding the liquid, which comes from food. This happens when the liquid rises to the outer wall of the heart and continues without stopping. There is always a constant flow of liquid that turns into blood, and the heart is where blood is first formed. We can see this in the early stages of life, as the heart contains blood before the veins become clear. This is why young people have faster pulses than older people, as there's more vapor being produced in the young.

All veins pulse at the same time because they are connected to the heart. Since the heart always beats, the veins also beat continuously and in sync with the heart.

So, palpitation is the heart's reaction to being squeezed by cold, while pulsation is caused by the heated liquid turning into vapor.

Respiration happens when the hot substance, which is the source of nutrition, grows. This part of the body needs more nutrition than other parts because it feeds them. As it grows, it makes the organ expand. This organ is built like a pair of bellows, similar to those used by blacksmiths. The heart and lungs have a similar shape. This structure must be double because the source of nutrition needs to be at the center of the natural forces.

As the organ expands, it causes the surrounding parts to rise. We can see this happen when people breathe. They lift their chest because the part inside the chest expands the same way. When this part expands, air rushes in like it would in bellows. The air is cold, so it cools the heat by reducing the excess fire. When the organ shrinks, the air that entered is pushed back out. When air enters, it's cold, but when it exits, it's warm because it has been in contact with the heat in the organ. This is especially true for animals with lungs full of blood. The lung has many tubes with blood vessels next to them, so it seems like the whole lung is full of blood. The movement of air inward is called respiration, and the movement outward is called expiration. This process continues for as long as the animal lives, as the organ keeps moving constantly. Life is tied to this constant movement of air in and out.

The movement of gills in fish happens in the same way. When the hot substance in the blood rises, the gills rise too and let water pass through. When the heat is cooled and flows back to the heart, the gills contract and push the water out. As the heat in the heart rises and then cools, this process repeats. So, just as breathing is tied to life and death in air-breathing animals, water entering and exiting is tied to life and death in fish.

We have now covered life, death, and related topics. But health and disease also deserve the attention of scientists, not just doctors, when it comes to understanding their causes. It's important to recognize the difference between the work of scientists and that of physicians, although they overlap in some ways. Doctors who are well-educated often mention natural science and claim that their methods come from it. On the other hand, the best scientists often take their studies so far that they end up discussing medical principles too.

• • •

The End

Thank you for Reading

Dear Reader,

We hope this timeless classic has sparked your imagination and enriched your literary journey. Now that you've turned the final page, we want to share a vision for the future of reading—one where every classic you've ever wanted to explore is at your fingertips, in a format that best suits your life.

We'd like to invite you to **gain immediate, unlimited digital & audiobook access** to hundreds of the most treasured literary classics ever written—along with the option to **secure deluxe paperback, hardcover & box set editions at printing cost**. Together, we can **spark a new global literary renaissance** alongside our small, independent publishing house called "The Library of Alexandria."

Thousands of years ago, the Library of Alexandria stood as a beacon of knowledge—until it was lost to history. We aim to reignite that spirit of preservation and discovery right now, in the modern age—only this time, it's accessible to all, in every language and every format.

Picture a world where every timeless classic, novel, poem, or philosophical treatise is not only available to read but also updated for today's readers—modernized, translated into any language or dialect, and ready to enjoy in any format you choose, whether that is in an eBook, audiobook, paperback, or deluxe hardcover & box set version a printing cost.

By joining our movement to **rebuild the modern Library of Alexandria**, you become part of an unprecedented mission to offer:

- **Unlimited Audiobook & eBook Access to the Greatest Classics of All Time**

  Instantly explore thousands of legendary works, from Plato and Shakespeare to Jane Austen and Leo Tolstoy. All are instantly ready to read or listen to, giving you a complete literary universe at your fingertips.

- **Paperback & Deluxe Editions at Printing Costs:**

  Purchase any title in a paperback, deluxe hardbound, or deluxe boxset edition at printing costs, shipped right to your doorstep. Curate your personal library of Alexandria with editions worthy of display—crafted to last, designed to captivate, and delivered straight to your door.

- **Modern translations for Contemporary Readers in all languages and dialects**

Discover a vast selection of classics reimagined in clear, current language—no more struggling with outdated phrases or obscure references. Next to the original versions, we aim to offer translations in as many languages and dialects as possible.

As we continue our translation efforts and add new languages, readers everywhere can connect with these works as if they were written today. ***By bridging linguistic divides, you're contributing to ensuring that these timeless stories become more meaningful, accessible, and inspiring for people across the globe.***

- **Your Personal Library of Alexandria:**

  Over the months and years, you'll curate a unique physical archive of classics—each volume a testament to your taste, curiosity, and love of knowledge. It's not just about owning books—it's about curating a cultural legacy you'll cherish and pass down for generations to come.

- **Join a Global Literary Renaissance:**

  Your support fuels an ongoing mission: allowing us to reinvest in offering deluxe print editions (including special boxsets) at their true cost, broaden the range of available formats and translations, and extend the reach of these works to new audiences worldwide.

By joining today, you're not just preserving a legacy of masterpieces; ***you set in motion a powerful wave of literary accessibility.***

We are more than a publisher—we're a movement, and we can't do it alone. Your support lets us scale our mission, preserving and reimagining history's greatest works for tomorrow's readers.

Become a Torchbearer of knowledge.

Thank you for picking up this book and allowing us into your literary journey. As you turn the pages, know that you're part of something larger: a global effort to keep these stories alive, share their wisdom across borders and generations, and spark a true cultural revival for the modern era.

If this resonates with you—please consider taking the next step. By visiting:
www.libraryofalexandria.com

With gratitude and a shared love of knowledge,

The Modern Library of Alexandria Team

Visit:

www.libraryofalexandria.com

Or scan the code below:

www.ingramcontent.com/pod-product-compliance
Lightning Source LLC
La Vergne TN
LVHW041943100826
845152LV00004B/64

* 9 7 8 1 8 0 4 2 1 4 0 3 9 *